Contents

Welcome to the Alan Rogers
'101' guides

The Alan Rogers guides have been helping campers and caravanners make informed decisions about their holiday destinations since 1968. Today, whether online or in print, Alan Rogers still provides an independent, impartial view, with detailed reports, on each campsite.

With so much unfiltered, unqualified information freely available, the Alan Rogers perspective is invaluable to make sure you make the right choice for your holiday.

101

best campsites
for walking & cycling

2014

alan
rogers

Compiled by: **Alan Rogers Travel Ltd**

Designed by: **Vine Design Ltd**

© Alan Rogers Travel Ltd 2013

Published by: **Alan Rogers Travel Ltd,
Spelmonden Old Oast, Goudhurst, Kent TN17 1HE**
Tel: **01580 214000** www.alanrogers.com

British Library Cataloguing-in-Publication Data:
A catalogue record for this book is
available from the British Library.

ISBN 978-1-909057-35-7

Printed in Great Britain by
Stephens & George Print Group

What is the '101' series?

At Alan Rogers, we know that readers have many and diverse interests, hobbies and particular requirements. And we know that our guides, featuring a total of some 3,000 campsites, can provide a bewildering choice from which it can be difficult to produce a shortlist of possible holiday destinations.

The Alan Rogers 101 guides are devised as a means of presenting a realistic, digestible number of great campsites, featured because of their suitability to a given theme.

This book remains first and foremost an authoritative guide to excellent campsites you should consider when looking for a camping holiday with plenty of scope for walking and/or cycling opportunities for a range of levels.

101 Best campsites
for walking and cycling

Among the most popular activities while camping are walking and cycling. It's not surprising when so many campsites are set amid glorious scenery and beautiful countryside.

This guide highlights 101 campsites which are all worth considering and short listing for your holiday walking or cycling excursions. All offer scenic routes, often directly from the campsite's own gates. Some are located right on official way marked paths or trails – an indication that you are certain to find some wonderful itineraries and lovely countryside.

Of course much depends on what kind of level you are expecting or wanting. Those looking for a rigorous daily workout and some serious exercise will have differing needs to those who fancy a little off-site exploration under their own steam while staying on the campsite.

One thing that is constant is the sense of quiet satisfaction that follows an excursion, however challenging, whether on wheels or on foot. After a leisurely ramble or a hard morning's pedal pushing, you return tired but having enjoyed new perspectives, and with a small sense of accomplishment.

Alan Rogers – in search
of 'the best'

Alan Rogers himself started off with the very specific aim of providing people with the necessary information to allow them to make an informed decision about their holiday destination. Today we still do that with a range of guides that now covers Europe's best campsites in 27 countries. We work with campsites all day, every day. We visit campsites for inspection purposes (or even just for pleasure!). We know campsites 'inside out'.

We know which campsites would suit active families; which are great for get-away-from-it-all couples; we know which campsites are planning super new pool complexes; which campsites offer a fantastic menu in their on-site restaurant; which campsites allow you to launch a small boat from their slipway; which campsites have a decent playing area for kicking a ball around; which campsites have flat, grassy pitches and which have solid hard standings.

We also know which are good for fishing, children, nature and outdoor activities; which are close to the beach; and which welcome dogs. These particular themes form our '101' series.

All Alan Rogers guides (and our website) are respected for their independent, impartial and honest assessment. The reviews are prose-based, without overuse of indecipherable icons and symbols. Our simple aim is to help guide you to a campsite that best matches your requirements – often quite difficult in today's age of information overload.

What is
the best?

The criteria we use when inspecting and selecting sites are numerous, but the most important by far is the question of good quality. People want different things from their choice of campsite, so campsite 'styles' vary dramatically: from small peaceful campsites in the heart of the countryside, to 'all singing, all dancing' sites in popular seaside resorts.

The size of the site, whether it's part of a chain or privately owned, makes no difference in terms of it being required to meet our exacting standards in respect of its quality and it being 'fit for purpose'. In other words, irrespective of the size of the site, or the number of facilities it offers, we consider and evaluate the welcome, the pitches, the sanitary facilities, the cleanliness, the general maintenance and even the location.

Expert
opinions

We rely on our dedicated team of Site Assessors, all of whom are experienced campers, caravanners or motorcaravanners, to visit and recommend campsites. Each year they travel around Europe inspecting new campsites for Alan Rogers and re-inspecting the existing ones.

When planning

your holiday...

A holiday should always be a relaxing affair, and a campsite-based holiday particularly so. Our aim is for you to find the ideal campsite for your holiday, one that suits your requirements. All Alan Rogers guides provide a wealth of information, including some details supplied by campsite owners themselves, and the following points may help ensure that you plan a successful holiday.

Find out more

An Alan Rogers reference number (eg FR 12345) is given for each campsite and can be useful for finding more information and pictures online at www.alanrogers.com. Simply enter this number in the 'Campsite Search' field on the Home page.

Campsite descriptions

We aim to convey an idea of its general appearance, 'feel' and features, with details of pitch numbers, electricity, hardstandings etc.

Facilities

We list specific information on the site's facilities and amenities and, where available, the dates when these facilities are open (if not for the whole season). Much of this information is as supplied to us and may be subject to change. Should any particular activity or aspect of the campsite be important to you, it is always worth discussing with the campsite before you travel.

Swimming pools

Opening dates, any charges and levels of supervision are provided where we have been notified. In some countries (notably France) there is a regulation whereby Bermuda-style shorts may not be worn in swimming pools (for health and hygiene reasons). It is worth ensuring that you do take 'proper' swimming trunks with you.

Charges

Those given are the latest provided to us, usually 2013 prices, and should be viewed as a guide only.

Toilet blocks

Unless we comment otherwise, toilet blocks will be equipped with a reasonable number of British style WCs, washbasins and hot showers in cubicles. We also assume that there will be an identified chemical toilet disposal point, and that the campsite will provide water and waste water drainage points and bin areas. If not the case, we comment. We do mention certain features that some readers find important: washbasins in cubicles, facilities for babies, facilities for those with disabilities and motorcaravan service points.

Reservations

Necessary for high season (roughly mid July to mid August) in popular holiday areas (i.e. beach resorts). You can reserve many sites via our own Alan Rogers Travel Service or through other tour operators. Remember, many sites are closed all winter and you may struggle to get an answer.

Telephone numbers

All numbers assume that you are phoning from within the country in question. From the UK or Ireland, dial 00, then the country's prefix (e.g. France is 33), then the campsite number given, but dropping the first '0'.

Opening dates

Dates given are those provided to us and can alter before the start of the season. If you intend to visit shortly after a published opening date, or shortly before the closing date, it is wise to check that it will actually be open at the time required. Similarly some sites operate a restricted service during the low season, only opening some of their facilities (e.g. swimming pools) during the main season; where we know about this, and have the relevant dates, we indicate it – again if you are at all doubtful it is wise to check.

Accommodation

Over recent years, more and more campsites have added high quality mobile homes, chalets, lodges, gîtes and more. Where applicable we indicate what is available and you'll find details online.

Special Offers

Some campsites have taken the opportunity to highlight a special offer. This is arranged by them and for clarification please contact the campsite direct.

Two legs good,
two wheels good

It's all part of the enduring appeal of camping: a relaxed way of life, lungfuls of clear, fresh air and beautiful countryside to explore. And how better to do so than on foot or on wheels. Whether you're looking for serious exercise or just want to get to know your surroundings, walking and cycling are a great solution.

Get Walking
and cycling

Walking and hiking are ever popular activities, being environmentally friendly and convenient. Cycle hire is often available (handy for collecting bread as well as exploring some beauty spots) and some campsites endeavour to make the most of their surroundings with marked trails.

Many campsites across Europe have invested heavily in impressive infrastructure and state of the art facilities. But simple enjoyment of the outdoor environment and a little curiosity about one's surroundings is all that is required to enjoy some walking and cycling while on holiday.

And if it prises the children away from the computer screen for a while then so much the better!

Why
do it?

Shape up!
Even on holiday, some people want to stay in trim. Others simply enjoy a little gentle exercise each day.

A unique viewpoint
When you're moving through the countryside under your own power, you have every chance to stop whenever you like. In a car the landscape flashes past, you don't see the details and you can't pause to savour something that catches your eye.

Small challenges
Enjoy that feeling of quiet satisfaction when you return from a challenging ride or a walk through the local forest, with only your pioneer map reading skills to bring you back to civilisation.

Learn about your natural surroundings
You're on holiday, your surroundings are unfamiliar; why not get out and explore? Enjoy getting to know the local flora and fauna.

It's free!
Apart from any special kit or hire charges, you can enjoy time with the family without paying handsomely for commercial attractions and the like. You'll also save on fuel costs.

alanrogers.com/walkingcycling

On
two legs

Walking is perhaps the simplest means of deriving pleasure while on holiday. It doesn't have to be strenuous - a walk through the adjacent meadows or into the village for an evening meal allows you to become a small part of local life for a while. And it's good for you too!

Walking
the walk

Being usually rurally located, you'll find many sites are geared up to encourage walkers. Some will even have walking notes and maps in reception for you to borrow and leaflets to help you spot local wildlife. Some take it to another level by organising accompanied rambles or hikes – these are generally excellent, giving you the chance to discover the best of the locality with the first-hand knowledge of a local.

Serious all-weather hikers might like to know which sites have special drying rooms for wet clothing and boots and which can provide packed lunches.

Walking
for health

Walking is an ideal exercise for maintaining health and fitness – it's low impact, low cost and requires no training!

Walking
to suit you

Explore the area

Very often campsites are bordered by fields, forest, seafront or even some kind of protected national park, so you'll often find paths that allow you to explore the neighbourhood.

Walking with a purpose

Many campsites are wonderfully located close to a magnificent château, a famous bridge, a stunning local view… Others are set just outside a village where a decent stroll takes you to local restaurants without the old debate of whose turn it is to drive.

Walking to wake up!

On a campsite it's always a pleasure to feel virtuous and walk to fetch the morning bread from the campsite shop, even on the largest sites, when you are pitched at the farthest point. It's part of the morning ritual and a pleasant start to the day, not a chore. It's about doing something a little different from the usual routine at home.

On
two wheels

Cycling is an activity all the family can take part in. Bikes loaded on the back of a 'van or roof of the car are a common site on the motorways across Europe during summer months. With bikes on board, there's always somewhere to go and a family outing was never more fun.

Cycling
made easy

Many sites offer a cycle hire service – often with a good range of well maintained bikes, of various sizes and with all the usual accessories. For some the expectation is only for occasional use – a potter around the local village, or an afternoon or two for the youngsters to cycle around the campsite. Elsewhere the approach is more serious, with some serious kit to suit different types of cycling, detailed route notes and guided tours with local itineraries.

Cycling for health

- An easy way to exercise
- Builds strength and muscle tone
- Improves stamina and general fitness
- Good for cardio-vascular fitness
- Helps weight loss
- Reduces stress

Cycling
to suit you

Mountain biking

The more challenging the terrain, the more likely this is going to be on offer – some sites in the rockier parts of the UK, Alps, Dolomites or Pyrenees offer some world-class terrain for the experienced mountain biker.

Road cycling

Outside the UK, road cyclists are treated with much more consideration and many competitive cyclists do head to the continent with the intention of some serious practice while on holiday. In fact, for some, the camping holiday is merely the means to an end.

Easy going trails

Possibly the largest group, recreational cyclists generally are after an easy going itinerary – it's gentle exercise rather than a punishing regime. They usually bike for the scenery and their bike rides are destination rides. They might spend a Saturday morning biking into the hills to see the autumn foliage, or cycling to a small craft fair to look around or pedalling along the trails in the local forest.

Enjoy...!

Whether you're an 'old hand' or are contemplating your first trip, a regular reader of our Guides or a new 'convert', we wish you well in your travels and hope we have been able to help in some way. We are, of course, also out and about ourselves, visiting sites, talking to owners and readers, and generally checking on standards and new developments. We hope to bump into you!

Wishing you thoroughly enjoyable camping and caravanning in 2014 – favoured by good weather of course!

The Alan Rogers Team

You
never know

Taking bikes and a pair of decent walking boots on a camping holiday will never be a bad idea. Even if you do not consider yourself a proper 'walker' you never know when you will be confronted by a once-in-a-lifetime spectacular view that cannot be ignored and yet which requires a bit of legwork to get to.

Equally, you might at any time come across an amazing bike trail, leading through superb scenery and crying out to be followed. The opportunities for enjoying some walking and cycling are all around you – don't miss out!

Facilities: Toilet facilities include a new fully equipped block, along with new facilities for disabled visitors and babies. Pleasant room with tables and chairs for poor weather. Laundry facilities. Shop (July-Sept). Swimming pool (Feb-Sept). Bar and cafeteria style restaurant (all year) serves a good value 'menu del dia' and snacks. WiFi in restaurant area (free). Play area. Fishing. Torches necessary in the new tent area. Off site: Riding 12 km. Bicycle hire 15 km. Golf and coast at Llanes 25 km.

Open: All year.

Directions: Avin is 15 km. east of Cangas de On's on AS114 to Panes and is best approached from this direction especially if towing. From A8 (Santander-Oviedo) km. 326 exit take N634 northwest to Arriondas. Turn southeast on N625 to Cangas and join AS114 (Covodonga/Panes) bypassing Cangas. Site is beyond Avin after 16 km. marker.

GPS: 43.3363, -4.94498

Charges guide

Per unit incl. 2 persons and electricity	€ 20,42 - € 26,06
extra person	€ 5,08 - € 5,40
child (4-14 yrs)	€ 4,05
electricity	€ 3,75

Spain – Avin-Onis

Camping Picos de Europa

E-33556 Avin-Onis (Asturias)
t: 985 844 070 e: adrian@picos-europa.com
alanrogers.com/ES89650 www.picos-europa.com

Accommodation: ✔ Pitch ✔ Mobile home/chalet ○ Hotel/B&B ✔ Apartment

This delightful site is, as its name suggests, an ideal spot from which to explore these dramatic limestone mountains on foot, by bicycle or on horseback. The site itself is continuously developing and the dynamic owner, José, and his nephew who helps out when he is away, are both very pleasant and nothing is too much trouble. The site is in a valley beside a pleasant, fast flowing river. The 160 marked pitches are of varying sizes and have been developed in three avenues, on level grass mostly backing on to hedging, with 6A electricity. An area for tents and apartments is over a bridge past the fairly small, but pleasant, round swimming pool. Local stone has been used for the L-shaped building at the main entrance which houses reception and a very good bar/restaurant. The site can organise caving activities, and has information about the Cares gorge along with the many energetic ways of exploring the area, including by canoe and quad-bike! The Bulnes funicular railway is well worth a visit.

You might like to know

The campsite reception is a mine of useful information about great hiking and mountain biking itineraries, with a good range of maps, books and personal experience!

- ✔ Walking notes or maps available
- ○ Waymarked footpath – direct access from site
- ✔ Waymarked footpath within 1 km. of site
- ○ Cycle trail – direct access from site
- ✔ Cycle trail access within 2 km. of site
- ○ Mountain bike track within 2 km. of site
- ○ Bicycle hire on site
- ○ Accompanied hiking trips
- ○ Accompanied cycling trips
- ○ Drying room for wet clothes/boots
- ○ Packed lunch service

Camping Peña Montañesa

Ctra Ainsa-Francia km 2, E-22360 Labuerda (Huesca)
t: 974 500 032 e: info@penamontanesa.com
alanrogers.com/ES90600 www.penamontanesa.com

Accommodation: ⊘ Pitch ⊘ Mobile home/chalet ○ Hotel/B&B ○ Apartment

A large site situated quite high up in the Pyrenees near the Ordesa National Park, Peña Montañesa is easily accessible from Ainsa or from France via the Bielsa Tunnel (steep sections on the French side). The site is essentially divided into three sections opening progressively throughout the season and all have shade. The 288 pitches on fairly level grass are of about 75 sq.m. and 10A electricity is available on virtually all. Grouped near the entrance are the facilities that make the site so attractive, including a fair sized outdoor pool and a glass-covered indoor pool with jacuzzi and sauna. Here too is an attractive bar/restaurant with an open fire and a terrace, a supermarket and takeaway are opposite. There is an entertainment programme for children (21/6-15/9 and Easter weekend) and twice weekly for adults in July and August. This is quite a large site which has grown very quickly and as such, it may at times be a little hard pressed, although it is very well run. The site is ideally situated for exploring the beautiful Pyrenees.

You might like to know

This site is a great base for many adventure sports including canyoning, potholing and mountain biking.

- ⊘ Walking notes or maps available
- ○ Waymarked footpath – direct access from site
- ⊘ Waymarked footpath within 1 km. of site
- ○ Cycle trail – direct access from site
- ⊘ Cycle trail access within 2 km. of site
- ○ Mountain bike track within 2 km. of site
- ⊘ Bicycle hire on site
- ⊘ Accompanied hiking trips
- ⊘ Accompanied cycling trips
- ○ Drying room for wet clothes/boots
- ○ Packed lunch service

Facilities: A newer toilet block, heated when necessary, has free hot showers but cold water to open plan washbasins. Facilities for disabled visitors. Small baby room. An older block in the original area has similar provision. Washing machine and dryer. Bar, restaurant, takeaway and supermarket (all 1/1-31/12). Outdoor swimming pool (1/4-31/10). Indoor pool (all year). Playground. Boules. Riding. Rafting. Only gas barbecues are permitted. Torches required in some areas. WiFi (free).
Off site: Fishing 100 m. Skiing in season. Canoeing nearby.

Open: All year.

Directions: Site is 2 km. from Ainsa, on the road from Ainsa to France.
GPS: 42.4352, 0.13618

Charges guide

Per unit incl. 2 persons
and electricity € 25,25 - € 33,70

Facilities: Two modern sanitary blocks include facilities for disabled visitors and laundry facilities. Supermarket. Bar, restaurant and takeaway (1/7-31/8). Swimming pools (15/6-15/9). Playground. Entertainment for children (high season). Pétanque. Guided tours, plus hiking, canyoning, rafting, climbing, mountain biking and caving. Bicycle hire. WiFi. No charcoal barbecues. Torches useful in some parts. Off site: Local bus service. Fishing 1 km.

Open: 15 January - 15 December.

Directions: South of the Park Nacional de Ordesa, site is 50 km. from Jaca near Ainsa. From Ainsa travel northwest on N260 toward Boltaña (near 443 km. marker) and 1 km. from Boltaña turn south toward Margudgued. Site is well signed and is 1 km. along this road.

GPS: 42.43018, 0.07882

Charges guide

Per unit incl. 2 persons and electricity € 35,40	
extra person € 6,50	
child (1-10 yrs) € 5,50	
dog € 3,25	

Camping Boltaña

Ctra N260 km. 442, E-22340 Boltaña (Huesca)
t: 974 502 347 e: info@campingboltana.com
alanrogers.com/ES90620 www.campingboltana.com

Accommodation: ✔ Pitch ✔ Mobile home/chalet ○ Hotel/B&B ○ Apartment

Nestled in the Rio Ara valley, surrounded by the Pyrenees mountains and below a tiny but enchanting, historic, hilltop village, is the very pretty, thoughtfully planned Camping Boltaña. Generously sized, 190 grassy pitches (all with 10A electricity) have good shade from a variety of trees and a stream meanders through the campsite. The landscaping includes ten charming rocky water gardens and a covered pergola doubles as an eating and play area. A stone building houses the site's reception, social room and supermarket. Angel Moreno, the owner of the site, is a charming host and has tried to think of everything to make his guests comfortable.

You might like to know

There are some excellent accompanied mountain bike trips into the spectacular Ordesa National Park.

- ✔ Walking notes or maps available
- ○ Waymarked footpath – direct access from site
- ✔ Waymarked footpath within 1 km. of site
- ○ Cycle trail – direct access from site
- ✔ Cycle trail access within 2 km. of site
- ✔ Mountain bike track within 2 km. of site
- ✔ Bicycle hire on site
- ○ Accompanied hiking trips
- ✔ Accompanied cycling trips
- ○ Drying room for wet clothes/boots
- ○ Packed lunch service

Facilities: Four modern, very clean and well equipped toilet blocks are built in traditional Portuguese style with hot water throughout. Washing machines. Motorcaravan services. Bar and restaurant (1/4-30/9). Shop (all year, bread to order). Lounge. Playground. Fishing. Boat hire. Tennis. Riding. Medical post. Car wash. Dogs are not accepted in July/Aug. Facilities and amenities may be reduced outside the main season. Off site: Swimming and boating in the lake.

Open: All year.

Directions: From A2 between Setubal and the Algarve take exit 10 on IP8 (Ferreira and Beja). Take road to Torrao and 13 km. later, 1 km. north of Odivelas, turn right towards Barragem and site is 3 km. after crossing head of reservoir following small signs.

GPS: 38.1812, -8.10293

Charges guide

Per unit incl. 2 persons and electricity € 25,70	
extra person € 5,80	
child (5-10 yrs) € 2,90	
electricity € 2,90	

Discounts of 10-20% outside June - Aug, and for longer stays. No credit cards.

Camping Markádia

Barragem de Odivelas, Apdo 17, P-7920-999 Alvito (Beja)
t: 284 763 141 e: markadia@hotmail.com
alanrogers.com/PO8350 www.markadia.net

Accommodation: ☑ Pitch ◯ Mobile home/chalet ◯ Hotel/B&B ◯ Apartment

A tranquil, lakeside site in an unspoilt setting, this will appeal most to those nature lovers who want to 'get away from it all' and to those who enjoy country pursuits such as walking, fishing and riding. There are 130 casual, unmarked pitches on undulating grass and sand with ample electricity connections (16A). The site is lit but a torch is required. The friendly Dutch owner has carefully planned the site so each pitch has its own oak tree to provide shade. The lake is in fact a 1,000-hectare reservoir, and more than 150 species of birds can be found in the area. The stellar views in the very low ambient lighting are wonderful at night. The bar/restaurant with a terrace is open daily in season but weekends only during the winter. One can swim in the reservoir, and canoes, pedaloes and windsurfers are available for hire. You may bring your own boat, although power boats, quads and motor scooters are not allowed on environmental grounds.

You might like to know

There are plenty of quiet walking and cycle tracks locally - the site's owners will be pleased to recommend routes.

- ☑ Walking notes or maps available
- ◯ Waymarked footpath – direct access from site
- ☑ Waymarked footpath within 1 km. of site
- ◯ Cycle trail – direct access from site
- ☑ Cycle trail access within 2 km. of site
- ◯ Mountain bike track within 2 km. of site
- ◯ Bicycle hire on site
- ◯ Accompanied hiking trips
- ◯ Accompanied cycling trips
- ◯ Drying room for wet clothes/boots
- ◯ Packed lunch service

Facilities: Three very clean sanitary blocks provide mixed style WCs, controllable showers and hot water. Good facilities for disabled visitors. Laundry. Gas supplies. Shop. Restaurant/bar. Outdoor pool (June-Sept). Playground. Bicycle hire. TV room (satellite). Medical post. Good tennis courts. Minigolf. Adventure park. Car wash. Barbecue areas. Torches useful. English spoken. Attractive bungalows to rent. WiFi in reception/bar area. Off site: Fishing, riding and bicycle hire 800 m.

Open: All year.

Directions: From north, N103 (Braga-Chaves), turn left at N205 (7.5 km. north of Braga). Follow N205 to Caldelas Terras de Bouro and Covide where site is signed to Campo do Gerês. An eastern approach from N103 is for the adventurous but with magnificent views over mountains and lakes.

GPS: 41.7631, -8.1905

Charges guide

Per unit incl. 2 persons and electricity € 13,60 - € 28,00	
extra person € 3,20 - € 5,50	
child (5-11 yrs) € 2,00 - € 3,30	
dog € 1,50 - € 3,00	

Parque de Campismo de Cerdeira

Rua de Cerdeira 400, P-4840 030 Campo do Gerês (Braga)
t: 253 351 005   e: info@parquecerdeira.com
alanrogers.com/PO8370 www.parquecerdeira.com

Accommodation: ◉ Pitch ○ Mobile home/chalet ○ Hotel/B&B ○ Apartment

Located in the Peneda-Gerês National Park, amidst spectacular mountain scenery, this excellent site offers modern facilities in a truly natural area. The national park is home to all manner of flora, fauna and wildlife, including the roebuck, wolf and wild boar. The well fenced, professional and peaceful site offers 600 good sized, unmarked, mostly level, grassy pitches in a shady woodland setting. Electricity (5/10A) is available for 200 of the 550 touring pitches, though some long leads may be required. A very large timber complex, tastefully designed with the use of noble materials – granite and wood - provides a superb restaurant with a comprehensive menu. A pool with a separated section for toddlers is a welcome, cooling relief in the height of summer. There are unlimited opportunities in the immediate area for fishing, riding, canoeing, mountain biking and climbing, so take advantage of this quality mountain hospitality.

You might like to know

There are some wonderful quiet lanes in the vicinity of the site – perfect for cycling or walking.

- ◉ Walking notes or maps available
- ○ Waymarked footpath – direct access from site
- ◉ Waymarked footpath within 1 km. of site
- ○ Cycle trail – direct access from site
- ◉ Cycle trail access within 2 km. of site
- ○ Mountain bike track within 2 km. of site
- ○ Bicycle hire on site
- ○ Accompanied hiking trips
- ○ Accompanied cycling trips
- ○ Drying room for wet clothes/boots
- ○ Packed lunch service

Facilities: The single rustic sanitary building has British style WCs with hot showers. It could be busy at peak periods. Washing machine. No facilities for disabled campers. No shop but just ask and the baker calls daily. Self-service bar with WiFi and library. Restaurant. Separate games and rest room with satellite TV. Artistic workshops. Swimming pool. Off site: Town with shops, bars and restaurants and bus service 1 km. Fishing and watersports 5 km. Riding 11 km.

Open: 1 February - 30 November.

Directions: From Lisbon take A1/A23 to Torres Novas then IC3 to Tomar and N238 to Ferreira do Zêzere. Take N348 to Vila de Rei and site is 1 km. from Ferreira do Zêzere to eastern side of town (do not enter town). From Coimbra use N238 road at an earlier exit.

GPS: 39.70075, -8.2782

Charges guide

Per unit incl. 2 persons and electricity	€ 16,25 - € 18,25
extra person	€ 3,50 - € 4,00
child (under 11 yrs)	€ 1,50 - € 2,00

Portugal – Ferreira do Zêzere

Camping Quinta da Cerejeira

Rua D. Maria Fernanda da Mota Cardoso 902, P-2240-333 Ferreira do Zêzere (Santarem)
t: 249 361 756 e: info@cerejeira.com
alanrogers.com/PO8550 www.cerejeira.com

Accommodation: ◉ Pitch ○ Mobile home/chalet ○ Hotel/B&B ◉ Apartment

This is a delightful, small, family owned venture run by Gert and Teunie Verheij. It is a converted farm (quinta) and has been coaxed into a very special campsite. The pitches are on flat grass or on long terraces under fruit and olive trees. There are 25 pitches of which 18 have access to 6A electricity (long leads may be needed). There is some shade and the site is full of rustic charm and craft works. It is very peaceful with views of the surrounding green hills from the charming vine-covered patio above a small swimming pool. You will notice the working well, no longer powered by a donkey but you can see where he used to circle to pump water. The charming restaurant offers a very reasonable menu of the day. Several rooms have been set aside for art and craft activities, and quality workshops are offered in a range of subjects including pottery, painting and Portuguese cooking. Live entertainment is organised in season. If you like a small, peaceful, friendly site this is for you.

You might like to know

A number of trails start at Quinta da Cerejeira, with others throughout Vila de Rei and in the Parque Natural das Serras de Aire e Candeeiros. Some routes are available for downloading on your GPS device.

- ◉ Walking notes or maps available
- ◉ Waymarked footpath – direct access from site
- ○ Waymarked footpath within 1 km. of site
- ○ Cycle trail – direct access from site
- ◉ Cycle trail access within 2 km. of site
- ○ Mountain bike track within 2 km. of site
- ○ Bicycle hire on site
- ○ Accompanied hiking trips
- ○ Accompanied cycling trips
- ○ Drying room for wet clothes/boots
- ○ Packed lunch service

Camping Arquin

Feldgatterweg 25, I-39011 Lana (Trentino - Alto Adige)
t: 0473 561 187 e: info@camping-arquin.it
alanrogers.com/IT61865 www.camping-arquin.it

Accommodation: ☑ Pitch ○ Mobile home/chalet ○ Hotel/B&B ○ Apartment

Camping Arquin is in the South Tirol (Alto Adige) where the majority of the population speak German. It is open from early March to mid November and lies in an open valley surrounded by orchards, beyond which are high mountains. This is a region of natural beauty and is famous for its flowery meadows. The site is close to the village of Lana, one of the largest in the South Tirol and famous for its Mediterranean climate. There are 120 sunny, level, grass pitches up to 100 sq.m, all with 6A electricity and many are fully serviced. There is a wide range of marked footpaths and cycling routes. This is a good base for active families wishing to explore the local area on foot, by bicycle, in the car, by bus or by train (Bolzano 20 km). The higher reaches of the mountains can be accessed by cable car. This area is also known for its thermal springs and baths. The interesting old town of Meran is only 7 km. away and is accessible by bus.

Facilities: Modern toilet block with all necessary facilities including those for babies and disabled visitors. Motorcaravan services. Small shop (15/3-5/11). Restaurant and bar (30/3-31/10). Small heated outdoor swimming pool (1/4-30/9). Play area. WiFi throughout (free). Charcoal barbecues not permitted. Off site: Bus stop 200 m. Large swimming pool 200 m. (May onwards; free to campers). Historical town of Meran 7 km. Museums. Golf and bicycle hire 2 km. Fishing 3 km. Hiking, Tennis. Paragliding. Rock climbing. Canoeing. Nature parks. Cable car.

Open: 1 March - 15 November.

Directions: Leave A22 Brenner motorway at Bozen Süd. Take expressway towards Meran. At the Lana-Burgstall exit turn left. After 250 m. take first right and follow signs to site.

GPS: 46.611151, 11.174434

Charges guide

Per unit incl. 2 persons
and electricity € 31,00 - € 35,00

dog no charge

You might like to know

Why not take the cable car to the summit of Vigiljoch to enjoy wonderful panoramic views and an excellent descent on foot?

- ☑ Walking notes or maps available
- ☑ Waymarked footpath – direct access from site
- ☑ Waymarked footpath within 1 km. of site
- ☑ Cycle trail – direct access from site
- ☑ Cycle trail access within 2 km. of site
- ☑ Mountain bike track within 2 km. of site
- ○ Bicycle hire on site
- ○ Accompanied hiking trips
- ○ Accompanied cycling trips
- ○ Drying room for wet clothes/boots
- ○ Packed lunch service

Facilities: The central toilet block is traditional but well maintained and clean. Additional facilities below the Residence are of the highest quality including individual shower rooms with washbasins, washbasins with all WCs, a delightful children's unit and an excellent facility for disabled visitors. Fully equipped private shower rooms for hire. Luxurious wellness centre with saunas, solarium, jacuzzis, massage, therapy pools and heat benches. Heated outdoor swimming and paddling pools. Play area. WiFi throughout (charged). Charcoal barbecues are not permitted. Off site: Tennis 800 m. Bicycle hire 1 km. Riding and fishing 3 km. Golf (9 holes) 10 km. Canoeing/kayaking 15 km.

Open: 6 December - 7 April, 8 May - 27 October.

Directions: Rasen/Rasun is 85 km. northeast of Bolzano. From Bressanone/Brixen exit on A22 Brenner-Modena motorway, go east on SS49 for 50 km. then turn north (signed Rasen/Antholz). Turn immediately west at roundabout in Niederrasen/Rasun di Sotto to site on left in 100 m.

GPS: 46.7758, 12.0367

Charges guide

Per unit incl. 2 persons, electricity on meter	€ 21,50 - € 32,50
extra person	€ 5,50 - € 8,20
child (3-15 yrs)	€ 3,00 - € 7,50
dog	€ 2,50 - € 4,20

Italy – Rasen

Camping Residence Corones

Niederrasen 124, I-39030 Rasen (Trentino - Alto Adige)
t: 047 449 6490 e: info@corones.com
alanrogers.com/IT61990 www.corones.com

Accommodation: ☑ Pitch ☑ Mobile home/chalet ○ Hotel/B&B ☑ Apartment

Situated in a pine forest clearing at the foot of the attractive Antholz valley, in the heart of German-speaking Südtirol, Corones is ideally situated both for winter sports enthusiasts and for walkers, cyclists, mountain bikers and those who prefer to explore the valleys and mountain roads of the Dolomites by car. There are 135 level pitches, all with 16A electricity and many also with water, drainage and satellite TV. The Residence offers luxury apartments and there are authentic Canadian log cabins for hire. The bar/restaurant and small shop are open all season. From the site you can see slopes which in winter become highly rated skiing pistes. A short drive up the broad Antholz/Anterselva valley takes you to an internationally important biathlon centre. An excellent day trip would be to drive up the valley and over the pass into Austria and then back via another pass. There is a regular programme of free excursions and occasional evening events are organised. Children's entertainment is provided in July and August.

You might like to know

Nature Fitness Park Kronplatz is Europe's largest Nordic Walking Park. There are 275 km. of well marked walking trails to be explored, with breathtaking views of the surrounding Dolomites.

- ☑ Walking notes or maps available
- ○ Waymarked footpath – direct access from site
- ☑ Waymarked footpath within 1 km. of site
- ○ Cycle trail – direct access from site
- ☑ Cycle trail access within 2 km. of site
- ☑ Mountain bike track within 2 km. of site
- ○ Bicycle hire on site
- ○ Accompanied hiking trips
- ○ Accompanied cycling trips
- ○ Drying room for wet clothes/boots
- ○ Packed lunch service

Facilities: One luxury underground block is in the centre of the site. 16 private units are available. Excellent facilities for disabled visitors. Fairy tale facilities for children. Infrared sensors, underfloor heating and gently curved floors to prevent slippery surfaces. Constant fresh air ventilation. Washing machines and large drying room. Sauna. Supermarket. Quality restaurant and bar with terrace. Entertainment programme. Miniclub. Children's adventure park and play room. Special rooms for ski equipment. Torches useful. WiFi (charged). Apartments and mobile homes for rent. Off site: Riding alongside site. 18-hole golf course (discounts) and fishing 1 km. Bicycle hire and lake swimming 2 km. ATM 3 km. Walks. Skiing in winter. Buses to cable cars and ski lifts.

Open: All year excl.
2 November - 20 December.

Directions: From A22-E45 take Bolzano Nord exit. Take road for Prato Isarco/Blumau, then road for Fie/Völs. Road divides suddenly – if you miss the left fork as you enter a tunnel (Altopiano dello Scilior/Schlerngebiet) you will pay a heavy price in extra kilometres. Enjoy the climb to Völs am Schlern and site is well signed.

GPS: 46.53344, 11.53335

Charges guide

Per unit incl. 2 persons	€ 21,10 - € 37,90
extra person	€ 7,00 - € 10,20
child (2-16 yrs)	€ 3,60 - € 8,10
electricity (per kWh)	€ 0,60
dog	€ 3,50 - € 5,20

Italy – Völs am Schlern

Camping Seiser Alm

Saint Konstantin 16, I-39050 Völs am Schlern (Trentino - Alto Adige)
t: 047 170 6459 e: info@camping-seiseralm.com
alanrogers.com/IT62040 www.camping-seiseralm.com

Accommodation: ☑ Pitch ☑ Mobile home/chalet ○ Hotel/B&B ☑ Apartment

What an amazing experience awaits you at Seiser Alm! Elisabeth and Erhard Mahlknecht have created a superb site in the magnificent Südtirol region of the Dolomite mountains. Towering peaks provide a wonderful backdrop when you dine in the charming, traditional style restaurant on the upper terrace. The 150 touring pitches are of a very high standard with 16A electricity supply, 120 with gas, water, drainage and satellite connections. Guests were delighted with the site when we visited, many coming to walk or cycle, some just to enjoy the surroundings. There are countless things to see and do here. Enjoy the grand 18-hole golf course alongside the site or join the organised excursions and activities. Buses and cable cars provide an excellent service for summer visitors and skiers alike. In keeping with the natural setting, the majority of the luxury facilities are set into the hillside. If you wish for quiet, quality camping in a crystal clean environment, then visit this immaculate site.

You might like to know

Alpe di Siusi is Europe's largest plateau with an altitude between 1,630 and 2,350 m. There are 350 km. of marked tracks with varying levels of difficulty.

☑ Walking notes or maps available
○ Waymarked footpath – direct access from site
○ Waymarked footpath within 1 km. of site
☑ Cycle trail – direct access from site
○ Cycle trail access within 2 km. of site
☑ Mountain bike track within 2 km. of site
○ Bicycle hire on site
○ Accompanied hiking trips
○ Accompanied cycling trips
○ Drying room for wet clothes/boots
○ Packed lunch service

Facilities: The two sanitary blocks are equipped to a high standard, one having been completely refurbished. They can be heated in cool weather. Shop, bar/pizzeria/restaurant with takeaway (11/4-30/10). Outdoor pool, with paddling pool (11/4-30/9). Smaller covered heated pool (11/4-30/10). Playground. No dogs in July/Aug. WiFi (free). Off site: Bicycle hire 300 m. Fishing 2.5 km. Riding 3 km.

Open: 5 April - 31 October.

Directions: Site is by the SS12 on northern edge of Leifers, 8 km. south of Bolzano. If approaching from north, at the Bolzano-Süd exit from A22 Brenner-Modena motorway follow Trento signs for 7 km. From south on motorway take Ora exit, then north on SS12 towards Bolzano for 14 km.

GPS: 46.25.48, 11.20.37

Charges guide

Per unit incl. 2 persons and electricity	€ 28,00 - € 35,00
extra person	€ 7,00 - € 9,00
child (under 9 yrs)	no charge - € 6,00

Less 10% for 2 weeks or more.

Italy – Laives/Leifers

Camping-Park Steiner

J. F. Kennedy Str. 32, I-39055 Laives/Leifers (Trentino - Alto Adige)
t: 047 195 0105   e: info@campingsteiner.com
alanrogers.com/IT62100   www.campingsteiner.com

Accommodation: ☑ Pitch ☑ Mobile home/chalet ☑ Hotel/B&B ○ Apartment

The welcoming Camping Steiner is very central for touring with the whole of the Dolomite region within easy reach. With much on-site activity, one could spend an enjoyable holiday here, especially now the SS12, by which it stands, has a motorway alternative. The 180 individual touring pitches, mostly with good shade and hardstanding, are in rows with easy access and all have 6A electricity. There are also 30 chalets available to rent. There is a family style pizzeria/restaurant, and indoor and outdoor pools. The Steiner Park Hotel provides another restaurant, café and full hotel facilities. This friendly, family run site has a long tradition of providing a happy camping experience in the more traditional style – the owner remembers Alan Rogers who stayed here on many occasions. We met a Danish couple during our visit who were staying for five weeks as it is so easy to get to different parts of the Dolomites and is ideal for walking.

You might like to know

You can cycle from Austria (Passo Resia or Passo del Brennero) to Lake Garda! You can also return by train to Camping Steiner.

☑ Walking notes or maps available
○ Waymarked footpath – direct access from site
☑ Waymarked footpath within 1 km. of site
○ Cycle trail – direct access from site
☑ Cycle trail access within 2 km. of site
☑ Mountain bike track within 2 km. of site
☑ Bicycle hire on site
○ Accompanied hiking trips
○ Accompanied cycling trips
☑ Drying room for wet clothes/boots
☑ Packed lunch service

Facilities: Four modern sanitary blocks
provide hot water for showers, washbasins
and washing. Mostly British style toilets.
Single locked unit for disabled visitors. Laundry
facilities. Freezer. Motorcaravan service point.
Good shop. Bar/restaurant and takeaway.
Outdoor swimming pool. Play area. Miniclub
and entertainment (high season). Fishing.
Satellite TV and cartoon cinema. Internet access
(free in low season). Kayak hire. Tennis. Torches
useful. Bicycle hire. Off site: Boat launching
500 m. Bicycle track 1.5 km. Town with all
the usual facilities and ATM 2 km. Riding 3 km.
Golf 7 km.

Open: 5 April - 12 October.

Directions: From A22 Verona-Bolzano road
take turn for Trento on S47 to Levico Terme
where campsite is very well signed.
GPS: 46.00799, 11.28454

Charges guide

Per unit incl. 2 persons and electricity	€ 9,50 - € 38,00
extra person	€ 3,00 - € 14,25
child (3-11 yrs)	no charge - € 6,50
dog	no charge - € 5,00

Italy – Levico Terme

Camping Lago di Levico

Localitá Pleina, I-38056 Levico Terme (Trentino - Alto Adige)
t: 046 170 6491 e: info@campinglevico.com
alanrogers.com/IT62290 www.campinglevico.com

Accommodation: ☑ Pitch ☑ Mobile home/chalet ○ Hotel/B&B ○ Apartment

Camping Lago di Levico, by a pretty lakeside in the mountains, is the merger of two popular
sites, Camping Levico and Camping Jolly. Brothers Andrea and Geno Antoniolli are making
great improvements, already there is an impressive new reception and further developments
of the lakeside and swimming areas are planned. The lakeside pitches are quite special.
There are 430 mostly grassy and shaded pitches (70-120 sq.m) with 6A electricity, 150 also
have water and drainage and 12 have private facilities. Staff are welcoming and fluent in
English. The swimming pool complex is popular, as is the summer family entertainment.
There is a small supermarket on site and it is a short distance to the local village. The
beautiful grass shores of the lake are ideal for sunbathing and the crystal clear water is ideal
for enjoying (non-motorised) water activities. This is a site where the natural beauty of an
Italian lake can be enjoyed without being overwhelmed by commercial tourism.

You might like to know

Various bikes are available for rent on
site, including high quality mountain
bikes. There is also a good repair and
maintenance facility.

- ☑ Walking notes or maps available
- ☑ Waymarked footpath – direct access from site
- ☑ Waymarked footpath within 1 km. of site
- ☑ Cycle trail – direct access from site
- ☑ Cycle trail access within 2 km. of site
- ☑ Mountain bike track within 2 km. of site
- ☑ Bicycle hire on site
- ☑ Accompanied hiking trips
- ☑ Accompanied cycling trips
- ○ Drying room for wet clothes/boots
- ○ Packed lunch service

Facilities: Excellent new sanitary blocks with British style toilets, free hot showers in generous cubicles. Small shop, bar, restaurant and takeaway (all 1/4-31/10). Communal barbecue. Entertainment area and pool near the sea. Tennis. WiFi over site (charged). High quality accommodation and tents for rent. Rocky beach at site. Dogs are not accepted in August. Off site: Small village of Finale 500 m. Riding 4 km. Larger historic town of Cefalu 12 km.

Open: All year.

Directions: Site is on the SS113 running along the northeast coast of the island, km. 172.9 just west of the village of Finale (the turn into site is at end of the bridge on the outskirts of the village). It is 12 km. east of Cefalu and 11 km. north of Pollina.

GPS: 38.02278, 14.15389

Charges guide

Per unit incl. 2 persons
and electricity € 27,00 - € 46,00

extra person (over 3 yrs) € 5,00 - € 10,00

Italy – Finale di Pollina

Camping Rais Gerbi

Ctra Rais Gerbi, SS113 km. 172.9, I-90010 Finale di Pollina (Sicily)
t: 092 142 6570 e: camping@raisgerbi.it
alanrogers.com/IT69350 www.raisgerbi.it

Accommodation: ☑ Pitch ☑ Mobile home/chalet ○ Hotel/B&B ○ Apartment

Rais Gerbi provides very good quality camping with excellent facilities on the beautiful Tyrrhenian coast not far from Cefalu. This attractive terraced campsite is shaded by well established trees and the 216 good sized pitches (6A electricity) vary from informal areas under the trees near the sea, to gravel terraces and hardstandings. Most have stunning views, many with their own sinks and with some artificial shade to supplement the trees. From the mobile homes to the unusual white igloos, everything here is being established to a high quality. The large pool with its entertainment area and the restaurant, like so much of the site, overlook the beautiful rocky coastline and aquamarine sea. Vincenzo Cerrito, who speaks excellent English, has been developing the site for many years and is continually upgrading and improving the resort-style facilities. Rais Gerbi is of special interest to fishermen – a local guide service is dedicated to sport fishing (sea and freshwater), even traditional squid fishing is available. During the spring and autumn the site is less busy.

You might like to know

Why not cycle to the small city of Cefalu, which is famous for its beautiful Norman cathedral and its sandy beach.

- ○ Walking notes or maps available
- ○ Waymarked footpath – direct access from site
- ○ Waymarked footpath within 1 km. of site
- ○ Cycle trail – direct access from site
- ○ Cycle trail access within 2 km. of site
- ○ Mountain bike track within 2 km. of site
- ☑ Bicycle hire on site
- ○ Accompanied hiking trips
- ○ Accompanied cycling trips
- ○ Drying room for wet clothes/boots
- ○ Packed lunch service

Facilities: Two sanitary blocks include toilets, washbasins and free hot showers. No facilities for disabled visitors. Washing machine and dryer. Baby room. Motorcaravan service point. Bar. Restaurant. Pizzeria. Well stocked shop. TV room. Bicycle hire. Tennis. Football and basketball pitch. New, comprehensive, well shaded children's play area. Entertainment (high season). WiFi (charged). Dogs are not accepted in July/Aug. Bungalows to rent. Off site: Sailing and boat launching 200 m. ATM in village. Riding 3 km. Golf 20 km. Costa Rei, Castiadas, Muravera, Villasimius.

Open: 1 April - 2 November.

Directions: Camping Capo Ferrato is in the southeast of Sardinia and can be reached by using the coast road towards Villasimius (SP17 or SS 125) then take the Costa Rei signs and the site is well signed on the southern edge of the village of Costa Rei. The site is in Costa Rei (Via delle Ginestre) and not on the promontory of Capo Ferrato.

GPS: 39.24297, 9.56941

Charges guide

Per unit incl. 2 persons
and electricity € 22,20 - € 52,90

extra person € 5,60 - € 13,20

child (3-12 jaar) € 4,00 - € 9,90

dog (excl. July/Aug) no charge

Special low season deals.

Italy – Muravera

Camping Capo Ferrato

Localitá Costa Rei, Via delle Ginestre, I-09040 Castiadas (Sardinia)
t: 070 991 012   e: info@campingcapoferrato.it
alanrogers.com/IT69770   www.campingcapoferrato.it

Accommodation: ☑ Pitch   ☑ Mobile home/chalet   ○ Hotel/B&B   ○ Apartment

Situated at the southern end of the magnificent Costa Rei, this small, friendly and well managed site has 83 touring pitches, many in great positions on the fine, white sand beachfront. They all have 3/6A electricity, are on sand, shady and of generous proportions. On the fringes of Costa Rei, the site benefits from close proximity to the shops and restaurants, yet enjoys absolute tranquillity. The charming restaurant holds it own against the village competition. This site is brilliant for beach lovers and windsurfers, and offers many watersports. It is reasonably priced and the beach shelves safely for children. The same family have been here since 1965 and the campsite was one of the first in Sardinia. In low season, special events are organised with other southern sites to enable you to 'feel the traditions' of Sardinia. Ask about the 'plein air' organisation.

You might like to know

The nearby Monte Sette Fratelli (seven brothers) Nature Park, a landscape of wooded canyons and Mediterranean vegetation, has well marked walking routes and is one of the few remaining homes of the Sardinian deer. The campsite has a Bike Centre for repairs and offers routes via GPS.

☑ Walking notes or maps available
○ Waymarked footpath – direct access from site
○ Waymarked footpath within 1 km. of site
○ Cycle trail – direct access from site
○ Cycle trail access within 2 km. of site
○ Mountain bike track within 2 km. of site
☑ Bicycle hire on site
☑ Accompanied hiking trips
☑ Accompanied cycling trips
○ Drying room for wet clothes/boots
☑ Packed lunch service

Facilities: One modern toilet block and a Portacabin style unit with toilets and controllable showers. Laundry with sinks. Bar/restaurant. Play field. Fishing (permit required). Torch useful. Off site: Riding 500 m. Bicycle hire 10 km.

Open: March - October.

Directions: Site is on the main Kranjska Gora-Bovec road and is well signed 3 km. east of Soca. Access is via a sharp turn from the main road and over a small bridge.
GPS: 46.33007, 13.644

Charges guide

Per person	€ 11,00 - € 13,00
child (7-12 yrs)	€ 5,50 - € 6,50
electricity	€ 3,50

Slovenia – Soca

Kamp Klin

Lepena 1, SLO-5232 Soca
t: 053 889 513 e: kampklin@siol.net
alanrogers.com/SV4235

Accommodation: ⦿ Pitch ⦿ Mobile home/chalet ○ Hotel/B&B ○ Apartment

With an attractive location surrounded by mountains in the Triglav National Park, Kamp Klin is next to the confluence of the Soca and Lepenca rivers, which makes it an ideal base for fishing, kayaking and rafting. The campsite has 50 pitches, all for tourers, with 7A electricity, on one large, grassy field, connected by a circular, gravel access road. It is attractively landscaped with flowers and young trees, which provide some shade. Some pitches are right on the bank of the river (unfenced) and there are beautiful views of the river and the mountains. Kamp Klin is privately owned and there is a 'pension' next door, all run by the Zorc family, who serve local dishes with compe (potatoes), cottage cheese, grilled trout and local salami in the restaurant. From the site it is only a short drive to the highest point of Slovenia, the Triglav mountain and its beautiful viewpoint with marked walking routes. Like so many Slovenian sites in this area, this is a good holiday base for the active camper.

You might like to know

There are some great walks in the surrounding mountains – something to suit all abilities.

⦿ Walking notes or maps available
⦿ Waymarked footpath – direct access from site
○ Waymarked footpath within 1 km. of site
○ Cycle trail – direct access from site
⦿ Cycle trail access within 2 km. of site
○ Mountain bike track within 2 km. of site
○ Bicycle hire on site
○ Accompanied hiking trips
○ Accompanied cycling trips
○ Drying room for wet clothes/boots
○ Packed lunch service

Facilities: Two attractive and well maintained log-built toilet blocks. Facilities for disabled visitors. Laundry facilities. Motorcaravan services. Shop (March-Nov). Café dispenses light meals, snacks and drinks apparently with flexible closing hours. Play area. Bowling. Fishing. Bicycle hire. Canoe hire. Climbing walls. Communal barbecue. WiFi. Off site: Town within walking distance. Riding 5 km. Golf 15 km. Guided tours in the Soca valley and around Slovenia start from the campsite.

Open: All year.

Directions: Approaching Kobarid from Tolmin on 102, just before Kobarid turn right on 203 towards Bovec and after 100 m. take descending slip road to right and keep more or less straight on to Napoléon's bridge (about 500 m). Cross bridge and site is on left, 100 m.

GPS: 46.25075, 13.58658

Charges guide

Per unit incl. 2 persons
and electricity € 25,00 - € 28,00

dog € 2,00

Slovenia – Kobarid

Kamp Koren Kobarid

Ladra 1b, SLO-5222 Kobarid
t: 053 891 311   e: info@kamp-koren.si
alanrogers.com/SV4270   www.kamp-koren.si

Accommodation: ⊘ Pitch   ⊘ Mobile home/chalet   ○ Hotel/B&B   ○ Apartment

Superbly run by its owner, Lidija Koren, this peaceful, well shaded site is located above the Soca river gorge in the countryside close to Kobarid. A small site with 90 pitches, it is deservedly very popular with those interested in outdoor sports, including hiking, mountain biking, paragliding, canoeing, canyoning, rafting and fishing. At the same time, its quiet location makes it a good site for those seeking a relaxing break. Six attractive, well equipped chalets are a recent addition. The Julian Alps, and in particular the Triglav National Park, is a wonderful and under-explored part of Slovenia that has much to offer. Kobarid, probably best approached via Udine in Italy, is a pleasant country town, with easy access to nearby rivers, valleys and mountains, which alone justify a visit to Kamp Koren. The local museum in Kobarid was recently voted European Museum of the Year and is excellent.

You might like to know

Top quality mountain bikes are available for rent. 2013 rates were € 15 per day and € 10 per half day.

- ⊘ Walking notes or maps available
- ○ Waymarked footpath – direct access from site
- ⊘ Waymarked footpath within 1 km. of site
- ○ Cycle trail – direct access from site
- ⊘ Cycle trail access within 2 km. of site
- ⊘ Mountain bike track within 2 km. of site
- ⊘ Bicycle hire on site
- ○ Accompanied hiking trips
- ○ Accompanied cycling trips
- ○ Drying room for wet clothes/boots
- ○ Packed lunch service

Camping Menina

Varpolje 105, SLO-3332 Recica ob Savinji
t: 035 835 027 e: info@campingmenina.com
alanrogers.com/SV4405 www.campingmenina.com

Accommodation: ⦿ Pitch ⦿ Mobile home/chalet ○ Hotel/B&B ○ Apartment

Camping Menina is in the heart of the 35 km. long Upper Savinja Valley, surrounded by 2,500 m. high mountains and unspoilt nature. It is being improved every year by the young, enthusiastic owner, Jurij Kolenc and has 200 pitches, all for touring units, on grassy fields under mature trees and with access from gravel roads. All have 6-10A electricity. The Savinja river runs along one side of the site, but if its water is too cold for swimming, the site also has a lake which can be used for swimming. This site is a perfect base for walking or mountain biking in the mountains. A wealth of maps and routes are available from reception. Rafting, canyoning and kayaking, and visits to a fitness studio, sauna and massage salon are organised. The site is now open all year to offer skiing holidays.

Facilities: Two toilet blocks (one new) have modern fittings with toilets, open plan washbasins and controllable hot showers. Motorcaravan service point. Bar/restaurant with open-air terrace (evenings only) and open-air kitchen. Sauna. Playing field. Play area. Fishing. Mountain bike hire. Russian bowling. Excursions (52). Live music and gatherings around the camp fire. Indian village. Hostel. Skiing in winter. Kayaking. Mobile homes to rent. Climbing wall. Rafting. Off site: Fishing 2 km. Recica and other villages with much culture and folklore are close. Indian sauna at Coze.

Open: All year.

Directions: From Ljubljana/Celje autobahn A1. Exit at Sentupert and turn north towards Mozirje (14 km). At roundabout just before Mozirje, hard left staying on the 225 for 6 km. to Nizka then just after the circular automatic petrol station, left where site is signed.

GPS: 46.31168, 14.90913

Charges guide

Per unit incl. 2 persons and electricity	€ 17,80 - € 23,00
extra person	€ 7,50 - € 10,00
child (5-15 yrs)	€ 3,50 - € 6,00
dog	€ 2,50 - € 3,00

You might like to know

Roads between the valleys around the site offer around 1000 km. combinations of cycle friendly routes. The site has a partnership with a cycling holiday organiser and various excursions are possible.

- ☑ Walking notes or maps available
- ○ Waymarked footpath – direct access from site
- ☑ Waymarked footpath within 1 km. of site
- ○ Cycle trail – direct access from site
- ☑ Cycle trail access within 2 km. of site
- ☑ Mountain bike track within 2 km. of site
- ☑ Bicycle hire on site
- ○ Accompanied hiking trips
- ☑ Accompanied cycling trips
- ○ Drying room for wet clothes/boots
- ○ Packed lunch service

Balatontourist Camping Füred

Széchenyi út 24., H-8230 Balatonfüred (Veszprem County)
t: 87 580 241 e: fured@balatontourist.hu
alanrogers.com/HU5090 www.balatontourist.hu

Accommodation: ✓ Pitch   ✓ Mobile home/chalet   ✓ Hotel/B&B   ✓ Apartment

Facilities: Five fully equipped toilet blocks around the site include hot water for laundry and dishwashing. Baby rooms. Private cabins for rent. Laundry service. Numerous bars, restaurants, cafés, food bars and supermarket (15/5-15/9). Stalls and kiosks with wide range of goods and souvenirs. Excellent swimming pool (1/6-31/8). Sandy beach. Large free water chute. Animation for children. Sports activities organised for adults. Sauna. Massage. Fishing. Water ski lift. Windsurf school. Sailing. Pedalos. Play area. Bicycle hire. Tennis. Minigolf. Video games. WiFi over site (charged). Dogs are not accepted. Off site: Close by a street of fast food bars (about ten in all), with terraces under trees, offer a variety of Hungarian and international dishes. Riding and golf 10 km.

Open: 27 April - 30 September.

Directions: Site is just south of Balatonfüred, at the traffic circle on Balatonfüred-Tihany road is well signed. Gates closed 13.00-15.00 except at weekends.

GPS: 46.94565, 17.87709

Charges guide

Per unit incl. 2 persons
and electricity HUF 3600 - 9300

extra person HUF 800 - 1600

child (2-14 yrs) HUF 500 - 1200

This is a large international holiday village rather than just a campsite. Pleasantly decorated with flowers and shrubs, it offers a very wide range of facilities and sporting activities. All that one could want for a family holiday can be found here. The 890 individual pitches (60-120 sq.m), all with electricity (6/10A), are on either side of hard access roads on which pitch numbers are painted. Many bungalows are for rent. Mature trees cover about two thirds of the site giving shade, with the remaining area being in the open. Directly on the lake with 800 m. of access for boats and bathing, there is a large, grassy area for relaxation, a small beach area for children and a variety of watersports. A water-ski drag lift is most spectacular with its four towers erected in the lake to pull skiers around the circuit. There is a swimming pool on site with lifeguards. Along the main road that runs through the site are shops and kiosks, with the main bar/restaurant and terrace overlooking the lake. Other bars and restaurants are around the site. Coach trips and pleasure cruises are organised.

You might like to know

Lake Balaton is Central Europe's largest lake and there are miles of excellent cycle tracks around much of its perimeter.

- ✓ Walking notes or maps available
- ◯ Waymarked footpath – direct access from site
- ✓ Waymarked footpath within 1 km. of site
- ◯ Cycle trail – direct access from site
- ✓ Cycle trail access within 2 km. of site
- ◯ Mountain bike track within 2 km. of site
- ✓ Bicycle hire on site
- ◯ Accompanied hiking trips
- ◯ Accompanied cycling trips
- ◯ Drying room for wet clothes/boots
- ◯ Packed lunch service

Balatontourist Camping Napfény

Halász ut. 5, H-8253 Révfülöp (Veszprem County)
t: 87 563 031 e: napfeny@balatontourist.hu
alanrogers.com/HU5370 www.balatontourist.hu

Accommodation: ☑ Pitch ☑ Mobile home/chalet ○ Hotel/B&B ○ Apartment

Camping Napfény, an exceptionally good site, is designed for families with children of all ages looking for an active holiday, and has a 200 m. frontage on Lake Balaton. The site's 370 pitches vary in size (60-110 sq.m) and almost all have shade – very welcome during the hot Hungarian summers – and 6A electricity. As with most of the sites on Lake Balaton, a train line runs just outside the site boundary. There are steps to get into the lake and canoes, boats and pedaloes for hire. An extensive entertainment programme is designed for all ages and there are several bars and restaurants of various styles. There are souvenir shops and a supermarket. In fact, you need not leave the site at all during your holiday, although there are several excursions on offer, including to Budapest or to one of the many Hungarian spas, a trip over Lake Balaton or a traditional wine tour.

You might like to know

This excellent site has a wide range of activities on offer, including canoeing and rowing as well as bicycle hire.

- ☑ Walking notes or maps available
- ○ Waymarked footpath – direct access from site
- ☑ Waymarked footpath within 1 km. of site
- ○ Cycle trail – direct access from site
- ☑ Cycle trail access within 2 km. of site
- ○ Mountain bike track within 2 km. of site
- ☑ Bicycle hire on site
- ○ Accompanied hiking trips
- ○ Accompanied cycling trips
- ○ Drying room for wet clothes/boots
- ○ Packed lunch service

Facilities: The three excellent, well equipped sanitary blocks have child-size toilets and washbasins. Two bathrooms (hourly charge). Heated baby room. Facilities for disabled visitors. Launderette. Dog shower. Motorcaravan services. Supermarket, souvenir shop and several bars (all 1/6-31/8). Restaurants. Children's pool. Massage. Hairdresser. Sports field. Minigolf. Fishing. Bicycle hire. Canoe, rowing boat and pedalo hire. Extensive entertainment programme for all ages. WiFi over site (charged). Off site: Riding 3 km. Golf 20 km.

Open: 27 April - 30 September.

Directions: Follow road 71 from Veszprém southeast to Keszthely. Site is in Révfülöp.
GPS: 46.829469, 17.640164

Charges guide

Per unit incl. 2 persons and electricity	HUF 3750 - 7050
extra person	HUF 900 - 1250
child (2-14 yrs)	HUF 550 - 1000
dog	HUF 550 - 1000

Facilities: The good toilet facilities in the main building include free preset hot water in washbasins, showers and sinks for laundry and dishes. Washing machine and dryer. Gas supplies. Shop (1/7-31/8, bread to order). Bar (1/6-30/9). Swimming pool and paddling pool (15/6-15/9). TV. Table football. Fishing in adjacent stream (licence from reception). Internet and WiFi. Off site: Bus to Chatel stops at the gate. Bicycle hire 3 km. Riding 10 km.

Open: 1 May - 30 September.

Directions: From motorway 12/E27 (Bern-Vevey) take Châtel St Denis exit no. 2 and turn towards Les Paccots (1 km). Site is on left up hill.

GPS: 46.52513, 6.91828

Charges guide

Per person	CHF 6,50
child (6-16 yrs)	CHF 4,50
pitch	CHF 16,50
electricity	CHF 4,50

No credit cards. Euros are accepted.

Switzerland – Châtel-Saint Denis

Camping le Bivouac

Route des Paccots 21, CH-1618 Châtel-Saint Denis (Fribourg)
t: 021 948 7849 e: info@le-bivouac.ch
alanrogers.com/CH9300 www.le-bivouac.ch

Accommodation: ☑ Pitch ○ Mobile home/chalet ○ Hotel/B&B ○ Apartment

A pleasant little site in the forested mountains above Montreux and Vevey on Lac Leman (Lake Geneva). Le Bivouac has its own small swimming pool and children's pool. Most of the places here are taken by seasonal caravans (130) interspersed with about 30 pitches for tourists. Electrical connections (10A) are available and there are five water points. Due to access difficulties, the site is not open to tourers in winter. The active can take mountain walks in the area, or set off to explore Montreux and the lake. Others will enjoy the peace and quiet of this green hideaway. M. Fivaz, the owner, speaks excellent English and is only too happy to suggest local activities.

You might like to know

This area offers a good selection of walks, generally of a fairly undemanding nature. Walking is the best way to appreciate the area fully, and it need not be too strenuous if combined with one of the mountain trains or cable-cars.

☑ Walking notes or maps available
☑ Waymarked footpath – direct access from site
○ Waymarked footpath within 1 km. of site
○ Cycle trail – direct access from site
☑ Cycle trail access within 2 km. of site
○ Mountain bike track within 2 km. of site
○ Bicycle hire on site
○ Accompanied hiking trips
○ Accompanied cycling trips
☑ Drying room for wet clothes/boots
○ Packed lunch service

Facilities:
Facilities: The well constructed, heated sanitary block is of good quality. Washing machine and dryer. Gas supplies. Motorcaravan services. Communal room with TV. Kiosk (1/7-31/8). Play area and play house. Mountain bike hire. Fishing. Bicycle hire. WiFi. Off site: Shops and restaurants 10 minutes walk away in village. Riding 2 km. Outdoor and indoor pools, tennis and minigolf in Frutigen. A new sauna and wellness centre has recently opened in the village. Skiing and walking.

Open: All year.

Directions: Take Kandersteg road from Spiez and leave at Frutigen Dorf exit from where site is signed.

GPS: 46.58173, 7.64219

Charges guide

Per unit incl. 2 persons and electricity	CHF 25,80 - 32,30
extra person	CHF 6,40
child (1-16 yrs)	CHF 1,50 - 3,20
dog	CHF 1,50

Camping Grassi

Grassiweg 60, CH-3714 Frutigen (Bern)
t: 033 671 1149 e: campinggrassi@bluewin.ch
alanrogers.com/CH9360 www.camping-grassi.ch

Accommodation: ☑ Pitch ○ Mobile home/chalet ○ Hotel/B&B ○ Apartment

This is a small site with about half the pitches occupied by static caravans, used by their owners for weekends and holidays. The 70 or so places available for tourists are not marked out but it is said that the site is not allowed to become overcrowded. Most places are on level grass with two small terraces at the end of the site. There is little shade but the site is set in a river valley with trees on the hills which enclose the area. Electricity is available for all pitches but long leads may be required in parts. It would make a useful overnight stop en route for Kandersteg and the railway station where cars can join the train for transportation through the Lotschberg Tunnel to the Rhône Valley and Simplon Pass, or for a longer stay to explore the Bernese Oberland.

You might like to know

This is a good starting point for mountain walks along the north or south wall of the Lötschbergbahn.

- ☑ Walking notes or maps available
- ☑ Waymarked footpath – direct access from site
- ○ Waymarked footpath within 1 km. of site
- ☑ Cycle trail – direct access from site
- ○ Cycle trail access within 2 km. of site
- ☑ Mountain bike track within 2 km. of site
- ☑ Bicycle hire on site
- ○ Accompanied hiking trips
- ○ Accompanied cycling trips
- ☑ Drying room for wet clothes/boots
- ○ Packed lunch service

Facilities:
Seven separate toilet blocks are practical, heated and fully equipped. They include free hot water for baths and showers. Twenty private toilet units are for rent. Laundry facilities. Motorcaravan services. Gas supplies. Excellent shop (1/4-15/10). Site-owned restaurant adjacent (1/3-30/10). Snack bar with takeaway (1/7-20/8). TV room. Playground and paddling pool. Minigolf. Bicycle hire. Sailing school. Lake swimming. Boat hire (slipway for campers' own). Fishing. Daily activity and entertainment programme in high season. Excursions. Max. 1 dog. WiFi (charged). Off site: Golf (18 holes) 500 m. (handicap card). Riding 3 km. Good area for cycling and walking. Free return bus and boat service to Interlaken's stations and heated indoor and outdoor swimming pools (free entry).

Open: All year.

Directions: Site is 3 km. west of Interlaken along the road running north of the Thunersee towards Thun. Follow signs for 'Camp 1'. From A8 (bypassing Interlaken) take exit 24 marked 'Gunten, Beatenberg', which is a spur road bringing you out close to site.
GPS: 46.68129, 7.81524

Charges guide

Per unit incl. 2 persons and electricity	CHF 37,00 - 63,50
extra person	CHF 10,50
child (6-15 yrs)	CHF 5,00
dog	CHF 4,00

Various discounts for longer stays.

Camping Manor Farm 1

Seestrassee 201, Unterseen, CH-3800 Interlaken-Thunersee (Bern)
t: 033 822 2264   e: info@manorfarm.ch
alanrogers.com/CH9420   www.manorfarm.ch

Accommodation: ⊘ Pitch   ⊘ Mobile home/chalet   ○ Hotel/B&B   ⊘ Apartment

Manor Farm has been popular with British visitors for many years, as this is one of the traditional touring areas of Switzerland. The flat terrain is divided into 500 individual, numbered pitches, which vary considerably, both in size (60-100 sq.m) and price. There is shade in some places. There are 144 pitches with electricity (4/13A), water and drainage, and 55 also have cable TV connections. Reservations can be made, although you should find space, except perhaps in late July/early August when the best places may be taken. Around 40 per cent of the pitches are taken by permanent or letting units and four tour operators. The site lies outside the town on the northern side of the Thuner See, with most of the site between the road and lake but with one part on the far side of the road. Interlaken is very much a tourist town, but the area is rich in scenery with innumerable mountain excursions and walks available. The lakes and Jungfrau railway are near at hand.

You might like to know
There are many excellent mountain railways in the area and good local bus connections throughout the year.

- ⊘ Walking notes or maps available
- ⊘ Waymarked footpath – direct access from site
- ○ Waymarked footpath within 1 km. of site
- ⊘ Cycle trail – direct access from site
- ○ Cycle trail access within 2 km. of site
- ○ Mountain bike track within 2 km. of site
- ⊘ Bicycle hire on site
- ○ Accompanied hiking trips
- ○ Accompanied cycling trips
- ⊘ Drying room for wet clothes/boots
- ○ Packed lunch service

Camping Lazy Rancho 4

Lehnweg 6, CH-3800 Unterseen-Interlaken (Bern)
t: 033 822 8716 e: info@lazyrancho.ch
alanrogers.com/CH9430 www.lazyrancho.ch

Accommodation: ☑ Pitch ☑ Mobile home/chalet ○ Hotel/B&B ○ Apartment

This super site is in a quiet location with fantastic views of the dramatic mountains of Eiger, Monch and Jungfrau. Neat, orderly and well maintained, the site is situated in a wide valley just 1 km. from Lake Thun and 1.5 km. from Interlaken. The English speaking owners lovingly care for the site and will endeavour to make you feel very welcome. Connected by gravel roads, the 155 pitches, of which 90 are for touring units, are on well tended level grass (some with hardstanding, all with 10A electricity). There are 28 pitches also with water and waste water drainage. This is a quiet, friendly site, popular with British visitors. The owners offer advice on day trips out, and how to get the best bargains on the railway.

You might like to know

There are many and varied hikes and mountain bike trails available throughout the Jungfrau region.

☑ Walking notes or maps available
☑ Waymarked footpath – direct access from site
☑ Waymarked footpath within 1 km. of site
☑ Cycle trail – direct access from site
☑ Cycle trail access within 2 km. of site
☑ Mountain bike track within 2 km. of site
☑ Bicycle hire on site
○ Accompanied hiking trips
○ Accompanied cycling trips
☑ Drying room for wet clothes/boots
○ Packed lunch service

Facilities: Two good sanitary blocks are both heated with free hot showers, good facilities for disabled campers and a baby room. Laundry. Campers' kitchen with microwave, cooker, fridge and utensils. Motorcaravan service point. Well stocked shop. TV and games room. Play area. Small swimming pool and hot tub (all season). Wooden igloos and bungalows for rent. Free WiFi. Free bus in the Interlaken area – bus stop is five minutes walk from site. Off site: Cycle trails and waymarked footpaths. Riding and bicycle hire 500 m. Golf 1 km. Fishing 1 km. Boat launching 1.5 km. Interlaken and leisure centre 2 km.

Open: 18 April - 20 October.

Directions: Site is on north side of Lake Thun. From road 8 (Thun-Interlaken) on south side of lake take exit 24 Interlaken West. Follow towards lake at roundabout then follow signs for campings. Lazy Rancho is Camp 4. The last 500 m. is a little narrow but no problem.

GPS: 46.68605, 7.830633

Charges guide

Per unit incl. 2 persons and electricity	CHF 30,50 - 54,50
extra person	CHF 6,00 - 8,00
child (6-15 yrs)	CHF 3,50 - 4,80
dog no charge -	CHF 3,00

Payment also accepted in euros.

Facilities: Three fully equipped modern sanitary blocks can be heated in winter and one provides facilities for disabled visitors. Baby baths. Laundry facilities. Motorcaravan services. Well equipped campers' kitchen. Excellent shop with photo printing facility. Self-service restaurant with takeaway (May-end Oct). General room with tables and chairs, TV, drink machines, amusements. Playgrounds and covered play area. Excursions and some entertainment in high season. Mountain bike hire. Internet point and WiFi. ATM. Drying room. Ski store. Off site: Free bus to ski station (in winter only).

Open: All year.

Directions: Go through Lauterbrunnen and fork right at far end (look for signpost) before road bends left, 100 m. before church. The final approach is not very wide.

GPS: 46.58807, 7.91077

Charges guide

Per person CHF 9,80 - 11,90

child (6-15 yrs) CHF 4,80 - 5,50

pitch incl. electricity (plus meter in winter) CHF 17,00 - 29,50

dog CHF 3,00

Camping Jungfrau

CH-3822 Lauterbrunnen (Bern)
t: 033 856 2010 e: info@camping-jungfrau.ch
alanrogers.com/CH9460 www.camping-jungfrau.ch

Accommodation: ☑ Pitch ☑ Mobile home/chalet ◯ Hotel/B&B ◯ Apartment

This friendly site has a very imposing and dramatic situation in a steep valley with a fine view of the Jungfrau at the end. It is a popular site and, although you should usually find space, in season do not arrive too late. A fairly extensive area is made up of grass pitches and hardcore access roads. All 391 pitches (250 for touring) have shade in parts, electrical connections (13A) and 50 have water and drainage also. Over 30% of the pitches are taken by seasonal caravans and it is used by two tour operators. Family owned and run by Herr and Frau Fuchs, you can be sure of a warm welcome and English is spoken. You can laze here amid real mountain scenery, though it does lose the sun a little early. There are many active pursuits available in the area, as well as trips on the Jungfrau railway and mountain lifts.

You might like to know

From the local railway station you can get to the Jungfraujoch station with some excellent walking opportunities en route.

- ☑ Walking notes or maps available
- ☑ Waymarked footpath – direct access from site
- ◯ Waymarked footpath within 1 km. of site
- ◯ Cycle trail – direct access from site
- ☑ Cycle trail access within 2 km. of site
- ◯ Mountain bike track within 2 km. of site
- ☑ Bicycle hire on site
- ◯ Accompanied hiking trips
- ◯ Accompanied cycling trips
- ☑ Drying room for wet clothes/boots
- ◯ Packed lunch service

Facilities: The main toilet block, heated in cool weather, is situated at the rear of the hotel and has free hot water in washbasins (in cabins) and (charged) showers. A new modern toilet block has been added near the top end of the site. Washing machines and dryers. Shop. Café/bar. Small lounge. Indoor pool complex. Ski facilities including a drying room. Large play area with a rafting pool fed by fresh water from the mountain stream. Torches useful. TV. WiFi. Golf. Off site: Golf driving range and 18-hole course nearby. Fishing and bicycle hire 1 km. Riding 2 km.

Open: All year.

Directions: From N2 Gotthard motorway, leave at exit 33 Stans-Sud and follow signs to Engelberg. Turn right at T-junction on edge of town and follow signs to 'Wasserfall' and site.
GPS: 46.80940, 8.42367

Charges guide

Per person CHF 6,90 - 11,00

child (6-15 yrs) CHF 4,25 - 5,50

pitch incl. electricity (plus meter)
CHF 10,00 - 17,00

dog CHF 2,00

Credit cards accepted (surcharge).

Camping Eienwäldli

Wasserfallstrasse 108, CH-6390 Engelberg (Unterwalden)
t: 041 637 1949 e: info@eienwaeldli.ch
alanrogers.com/CH9570 www.eienwaeldli.ch

Accommodation: ☑ Pitch ☑ Mobile home/chalet ☑ Hotel/B&B ○ Apartment

This super site has facilities which must make it one of the best in Switzerland. It is situated in a beautiful location, 3,500 feet above sea level, surrounded by mountains on the edge of the delightful village of Engelberg. Half of the site is taken up by static caravans which are grouped together at one side. The camping area is in two parts – nearest the entrance there are 57 hardstandings for caravans and motorcaravans, all with electricity (metered), and beyond this is a flat meadow for about 70 tents. Reception can be found in the very modern foyer of the Eienwäldli Hotel which also houses the indoor pool, health complex, shop and café/bar. The indoor pool has been most imaginatively rebuilt as a Felsenbad spa bath with adventure pool, steam and relaxing grottoes, Kneipp's cure, children's pool with water slides, solarium, Finnish sauna and eucalyptus steam bath (charged for).

You might like to know

A great variety of walks are available in the area, making good use of the excellent mountain railway and cable car network.

- ☑ Walking notes or maps available
- ☑ Waymarked footpath – direct access from site
- ○ Waymarked footpath within 1 km. of site
- ○ Cycle trail – direct access from site
- ☑ Cycle trail access within 2 km. of site
- ☑ Mountain bike track within 2 km. of site
- ○ Bicycle hire on site
- ☑ Accompanied hiking trips
- ○ Accompanied cycling trips
- ☑ Drying room for wet clothes/boots
- ○ Packed lunch service

Facilities: Three sanitary units of exceptional quality are heated when necessary. The newest unit has super facilities for children and wide access for disabled visitors. Hot water is free in all washbasins (some in cabins), showers and sinks. British style WCs. Washing machines and dryers in each block, one block has a drying room, another a baby room. Gas supplies. Motorcaravan services. Small shop. Recreation room with TV. Playground. WiFi (charged). Torches and long leads may be useful. Off site: Adventure park 100 m. Shops and restaurants 500 m. Riding 8 km. Bicycle hire 20 km.

Open: 15 May - 30 September.

Directions: Leave Martigny-Gd St Bernard road (no. 21/E27) to the right where signed Orsieres/La Fouly. Site is signed on right at end of La Fouly village. Take care along narrow access road.

GPS: 45.03347, 7.09367

Charges guide

Per unit incl. 2 persons
and electricity CHF 28,40 - 35,50

extra person CHF 8,00

child (2-12 yrs) CHF 4,00

dog CHF 3,00

Less 20% in May, June and September.

Switzerland – La Fouly

Camping des Glaciers

CH-1944 La Fouly (Valais)
t: 027 783 1826   e: info@camping-glaciers.ch
alanrogers.com/CH9660   www.camping-glaciers.ch

Accommodation: ☑ Pitch   ☑ Mobile home/chalet   ○ Hotel/B&B   ○ Apartment

Camping des Glaciers is set amidst magnificent mountain scenery in a peaceful location in the beautiful Ferret Valley, 1,600 m. above sea level (care is needed with long units). The site offers some pitches in an open, undulating meadow and the rest are level, individual plots of varying sizes in small clearings, between bushes and shrubs or under tall pines. Most of the 220 pitches have 10A electricity. M. Alain Darbellay has now taken over the reins from his mother, who ran the site for 40 years, and he intends to maintain the strong family interest and friendships built up over the years. Additional land has been added to increase the number of pitches available. This is a site for those seeking relaxation in pure, fresh mountain air or boundless opportunities for mountain walking. Marked tracks bring the Grand Saint Bernard Pass and the path around Mont Blanc within range, in addition to many others, with an abundance of flora and fauna for added interest. The local bus links to Orsieres, then trains to the old Roman city of Martigny.

You might like to know

Mountain bike hire is available at a number of locations in Verbier, with miles of trails on offer.

☑ Walking notes or maps available
☑ Waymarked footpath – direct access from site
○ Waymarked footpath within 1 km. of site
☑ Cycle trail – direct access from site
☑ Cycle trail access within 2 km. of site
○ Mountain bike track within 2 km. of site
○ Bicycle hire on site
☑ Accompanied hiking trips
○ Accompanied cycling trips
☑ Drying room for wet clothes/boots
○ Packed lunch service

Camping de Molignon

Route de Molignon, 163, CH-1984 Les Haudères (Valais)
t: 027 283 1240 e: info@molignon.ch
alanrogers.com/CH9670 www.molignon.ch

Accommodation: ☑ Pitch ☑ Mobile home/chalet ○ Hotel/B&B ○ Apartment

Camping de Molignon, surrounded by mountains, is a peaceful haven 1,450 m. above sea level. The rushing stream at the bottom of the site and the sound of cow bells and birdsong are likely to be the only disturbing factors in summer. The 100 pitches for tourists (75 with 10A electricity) are on well tended terraces leading down to the river. Excellent English is spoken by the owner's son who is now running the site. He is always pleased to give information on all that is available from the campsite. The easy uphill drive from Sion in the Rhône Valley is enhanced by ancient villages and the Pyramids of Euseigne. These unusual structures, cut out by erosion from masses of morainic debris, have been saved from destruction by their unstable rocky crowns. Although this is essentially a place for mountain walking (guided tours available), climbing and relaxing, there is a geological museum in Les Haudères, which has links with a British university. Cheese making and attractive flora and fauna add interest for those wishing to explore the area.

You might like to know

Over 100 km. of mountain bike trails (bicycle hire is available 1 km. from the site).

☑ Walking notes or maps available
☑ Waymarked footpath – direct access from site
○ Waymarked footpath within 1 km. of site
○ Cycle trail – direct access from site
☑ Cycle trail access within 2 km. of site
☑ Mountain bike track within 2 km. of site
○ Bicycle hire on site
☑ Accompanied hiking trips
○ Accompanied cycling trips
☑ Drying room for wet clothes/boots
○ Packed lunch service

Facilities: Two fully equipped sanitary blocks, heated in cool weather, with free hot showers. Baby room. Washing machines and dryer. Kitchen for hikers. Motorcaravan services. Gas supplies. Shop for basic supplies (15/6-15/9). Restaurant. Heated swimming pool with cover for cool weather (6x12 m). Sitting room for games and reading. Playground. Guided walks, climbing, geological museum, winter skiing. Fishing. Off site: Tennis and hang-gliding near. Ski and sports gear hire 1 km. Bicycle hire 1 km. Riding 1.5 km. Langlauf in winter.

Open: All year.

Directions: Leave the motorway at exit 27 and follow signs southwards from Sion for the Val d'Herens through Evolène to Les Haudères where site is signed on the right at the beginning of the village.
GPS: 46.09003, 7.50722

Charges guide

Per unit incl. 2 persons
and electricity CHF 22,65 - 34,40

extra person CHF 4,65 - 7,20

child (4-16 yrs) CHF 2,55 - 4,00

dog CHF 2,05 - 3,20

Less 10% in low season.

Facilities: The large sanitary block has underfloor heating, some private cabins, plus excellent facilities for babies, children and disabled visitors. Laundry facilities. Motorcaravan services. Fridge box hire. Bar. Restaurant and takeaway with at least one open all year. Pizzeria. Good shop. Playgrounds. Children's activity programme. Child minding (day nursery) in high season. Sports field. Archery. Youth room with games, pool and billiards. TV room with Sky. Open-air cinema. Mountain bike hire. Aquapark (1/5-30/9). Surf bikes and pedaloes. Canoes and mini sailboats for rent. Fishing. Extensive daily entertainment programme (mid May-mid Oct). Dogs are not accepted in high season (July/Aug). WiFi (charged). Off site: Tennis and minigolf nearby. Riding 6 km. Golf 12 km.

Open: All year.

Directions: From Inntal autobahn (A12) take Brenner autobahn (A13) as far as Innsbruck-sud/Natters exit (no. 3). Turn left by Shell petrol station onto B182 to Natters. At roundabout take first exit and immediately right again and follow signs to site 4 km. Do not use sat nav for final approach to site, follow camping signs.

GPS: 47.23755, 11.34201

Charges guide

Per unit incl. 2 persons and electricity € 24,45 - € 33,25	
extra person € 6,10 - € 9,00	
child (under 13 yrs) € 4,80 - € 6,50	
dog (excl. July/Aug) € 4,50 - € 5,00	

Special weekly, winter, summer and Christmas packages.

Ferienparadies Natterer See

Natterer See 1, A-6161 Natters (Tirol)
t: 051 254 6732 e: info@natterersee.com
alanrogers.com/AU0060 www.natterersee.com

Accommodation: ☑ Pitch ◯ Mobile home/chalet ◯ Hotel/B&B ☑ Apartment

In a quiet location arranged around two lakes and set amidst beautiful alpine scenery, this site founded in 1930 is renowned as one of Austria's top sites. Over the last few years many improvements have been carried out and pride of place goes to the innovative, award-winning, multifunctional building at the entrance to the site. This contains all of the sanitary facilities expected of a top site, including a special section for children, private bathrooms to rent and also a dog bath. The reception, shop, café/bar/bistro and cinema are on the ground floor, and on the upper floor is a panoramic lounge. Almost all of the 235 pitches are for tourers. They are terraced, set on gravel/grass, all have electricity and most offer a view of the mountains. The site's lakeside restaurant with bar and large terrace has a good menu. With a bus every hour and the city centre only 19 minutes away this is also a good site from which to visit Innsbruck. The Innsbruck Card is available at reception and allows free bus transport in the city, free entry to museums and a cable car trip.

You might like to know

A free shuttle bus is available for some accompanied walks, and hiking boots and day packs are also available for hire.

- ☑ Walking notes or maps available
- ☑ Waymarked footpath – direct access from site
- ◯ Waymarked footpath within 1 km. of site
- ☑ Cycle trail – direct access from site
- ◯ Cycle trail access within 2 km. of site
- ☑ Mountain bike track within 2 km. of site
- ☑ Bicycle hire on site
- ☑ Accompanied hiking trips
- ☑ Accompanied cycling trips
- ☑ Drying room for wet clothes/boots
- ◯ Packed lunch service

Facilities: The sanitary facilities are first class and include ten bathrooms to rent for private use. Baby room. Facilities for disabled visitors. Dog shower. Washing machine and dryer. Ski room. Motorcaravan service point. Small shop. Fresh bread each morning. Good value restaurant. New lakeside playground. WiFi over site (charged). Bicycle hire. Fishing. Apartments to rent. Renovated fitness and play rooms. Off site: Tiroler farmhouse museum 1 km. Kramsach 3 km. Rottenberg 4 km. Swarovski Kristallwelten. Zillertal. Innsbruck. Kufstein.

Open: All year.

Directions: From the A12 take Kramsach exit and follow signs for Zu den Seen past Camping Krummsee and Stadlerhof along northern shore of lake, then right at the crossroads. All clearly signed. Camping Seehof (300 m) is the first campsite you reach. New driveway and reception on the left.

GPS: 47.46196, 11.90713

Charges guide

Per unit incl. 2 persons and electricity	€ 17,30 - € 26,30
extra person	€ 4,60 - € 6,90
child (2-14 yrs)	€ 3,00 - € 4,50
dog	€ 3,00 - € 3,50

Austria – Kramsach

Camping Seehof

Reintalersee, Moosen 42, A-6233 Kramsach (Tirol)
t: 053 376 3541   e: info@camping-seehof.com
alanrogers.com/AU0065   www.camping-seehof.com

Accommodation: ◉ Pitch ○ Mobile home/chalet ○ Hotel/B&B ◉ Apartment

Camping Seehof is a family run site and excellent in every respect. It is situated in a marvellous, sunny and peaceful location on the eastern shores of the Reintalersee. The site's comfortable restaurant has a terrace with lake and mountain views and serves local dishes as well as homemade cakes and ice cream. The site is in two areas: a small one next to the lake is ideal for sunbathing, the other larger one adjoins the excellent sanitary block. There are 170 pitches, 130 of which are for touring (20 tent pitches), served by good access roads and with 16A electricity (Europlug) and TV points; 120 pitches are fully serviced, with more being upgraded every year. Seehof provides an ideal starting point for walking, cycling and riding (with a riding stable nearby) and skiing in winter. The Alpbachtal Seenland card is available without cost at reception and allows free bus transport and free daily entry to many worthwhile attractions in the region. With easy access from the A12 autobahn the site is also a useful overnight stop.

You might like to know

This is a great site for winter holidays with cross-country skiing adjacent and a free shuttle bus to the slopes.

- ◉ Walking notes or maps available
- ○ Waymarked footpath – direct access from site
- ◉ Waymarked footpath within 1 km. of site
- ○ Cycle trail – direct access from site
- ◉ Cycle trail access within 2 km. of site
- ○ Mountain bike track within 2 km. of site
- ◉ Bicycle hire on site
- ○ Accompanied hiking trips
- ○ Accompanied cycling trips
- ◉ Drying room for wet clothes/boots
- ○ Packed lunch service

Facilities: The sanitary facilities are of a very high standard, with private cabins and good facilities for disabled visitors. Baby room. Washing machine. Dog shower. Small shop (all year). Bar, restaurant and takeaway (15/5-30/9; Christmas to Easter). Play room. Ski room. Play area. Children's entertainment. Guided walks. Free shuttle bus to ski slopes. Bicycle hire. Slipway for canoes/kayaks. WiFi over site. Off site: Riding 1 km. Indoor pool at Feichten, Pilgrim's Church at Kaltenbrunn. Kaunertaler Glacier.

Open: All year.

Directions: From E60/A12 exit at Landeck and follow the B315 (direction Reschenpass) turn south onto the B180 signed Bregenz, Arlberg, Innsbruck and Fern Pass for 11 km. to Prutz. Site is signed to the right from the B180 over the bridge.

GPS: 47.08033, 10.659698

Charges guide

Per unit incl. 2 persons and electricity	€ 17,00 - € 27,00
extra person	€ 4,20 - € 7,50
child (5-17 yrs)	€ 3,80 - € 6,20
dog	€ 2,00 - € 3,00

Austria – Prutz

Aktiv-Camping Prutz Tirol

Pontlatzstrasse 22, A-6522 Prutz (Tirol)
t: 054 722 648   e: info@aktiv-camping.at
alanrogers.com/AU0155   www.aktiv-camping.at

Accommodation: ◉ Pitch   ○ Mobile home/chalet   ○ Hotel/B&B   ○ Apartment

Aktiv-Camping is a long site which lies beside, but is fenced off from, the River Inn. The 115 touring pitches, mainly gravelled for motorcaravans, are on level ground and average 80 sq.m. They all have 6A electrical connections, adequate water points, and in the larger area fit together somewhat informally. As a result, the site can sometimes have the appearance of being quite crowded. This is an attractive area with many activities in both summer and winter for all age groups. You may well consider using this site not just as an overnight stop, but also for a longer stay. From Roman times onwards, when the Via Augusta passed through, this border region's strategic importance has left behind many fortifications that today feature among its many tourist attractions. Others include rambling, cycling and mountain biking, swimming in lakes and pools as well as interesting, educational and adventurous activities for children. The Tiroler Summer card, available without charge at reception, has free offers and discounts for many attractions.

You might like to know

The Tirol is known mostly for its wonderful mountain scenery and seemingly unlimited hiking potential. There are plenty of straightforward options for beginners and rather more ambitious routes for experts.

- ◉ Walking notes or maps available
- ○ Waymarked footpath – direct access from site
- ◉ Waymarked footpath within 1 km. of site
- ○ Cycle trail – direct access from site
- ◉ Cycle trail access within 2 km. of site
- ◉ Mountain bike track within 2 km. of site
- ◉ Bicycle hire on site
- ◉ Accompanied hiking trips
- ◉ Accompanied cycling trips
- ◉ Drying room for wet clothes/boots
- ○ Packed lunch service

Facilities: Three attractive, modern sanitary units built with plenty of glass and wood, give good provision of all facilities. The newest (2013) includes large family bathrooms (free with certain pitches, to rent in the winter), a recreation and conference room and a fitness centre. Saunas, steam bath, massage, fitness room. Separate drying facilities for canoeists. Ski and equipment room. Motorcaravan service point. Shop, restaurant and bar. WiFi throughout (charged). Playground. Games room. Children's playroom. Watersports. Bicycle hire. Cabins to rent. Hotel and B&B accommodation. Off site: Cross-country track 300 m. Swimming pools at Lofer (July/August) 1 km. Skiing at Lofer Alm 2 km. Gorges and caves 5-7 km. Golf and riding 15 km. Salzburg 40 minutes drive. Many marked walking and cycling trails. Mountain climbing.

Open: All year excl. November.

Directions: From A12 exit 17 (south of Kufstein) take B178 east to St Johann in Tyrol, then continue on B178 to Lofer, then south on B311 towards Zell am See. Site is 200 m. after Lagerhaus filling station on left.
GPS: 47.57427, 12.70602

Charges guide

Per unit incl. 2 persons and electricity	€ 19,00 - € 32,50
extra person	€ 6,30 - € 8,50
child (under 15 yrs)	€ 5,00 - € 8,50
dog (max. 2)	€ 3,50

No credit cards.

Austria – Saint Martin bei Lofer

Park Grubhof

Nr. 39, A-5092 Saint Martin bei Lofer (Salzburg)
t: 065 888 237   e: home@grubhof.com
alanrogers.com/AU0265   www.grubhof.com

Accommodation: ✔ Pitch   ✔ Mobile home/chalet   ✔ Hotel/B&B   ✔ Apartment

Park Grubhof is a well organised, level and spacious site set in the former riding and hunting park of the 14th century Schloss Grubhof. The 200 pitches all with 12A electricity, have been carefully divided into separate areas for different types of visitor – dog owners, young people, families and groups, and a quiet area. There are 150 very large pitches, all with electricity, water and drainage, many along the bank of the Saalach river. Although new, the central building has been built in traditional Tirolean style. On the ground floor you will find reception, a cosy café/bar and a small shop, and on the first floor, a super sauna and wellness suite, two apartments and a relaxation room. Some areas are wooded with plenty of shade, others are more open and there are some very attractive log cabins which have been rescued from the old logging camps. Many of the possible activities are based around the river, where you will find barbecue areas, canoeing and white water rafting, fishing and swimming (when the river level reduces). The ski resort of Lofer Alm is only 2 km. away.

You might like to know

Walking and cycling at Grubhof offers treks into the Berchtesgaden National Park, flat cycle paths along the river or ambitious MTB tours – everything is on your doorstep. A warm welcome awaits at this spacious site set in spectacular, unspoilt countryside.

- ✔ Walking notes or maps available
- ✔ Waymarked footpath – direct access from site
- ○ Waymarked footpath within 1 km. of site
- ✔ Cycle trail – direct access from site
- ✔ Cycle trail access within 2 km. of site
- ✔ Mountain bike track within 2 km. of site
- ○ Bicycle hire on site
- ✔ Accompanied hiking trips
- ✔ Accompanied cycling trips
- ✔ Drying room for wet clothes/boots
- ○ Packed lunch service

Facilities: Three toilet blocks (one completely rebuilt for 2009), provide all the necessary facilities. Washing machines and dryers. Motorcaravan services. Restaurant (1/5-30/9, also open to the public). Takeaway. Bread. Swimming pool area with water slide. Jacuzzi, protected children's pool (open to public in afternoons). New playgrounds, games and animal park. Bouncy castle, trampoline. Outdoor fitness machines. Games room. Tennis. Pétanque. Bicycle hire. Discos, picnics, musical evenings. WiFi over site (charged, free in bar). Max. 2 dogs. Off site: Shop 500 m. in village. Fishing 5 km. Riding 10 km. Walking tours. Walibi theme park nearby.

Open: 1 April - 10 October.

Directions: Site signed from D931 Agen-Condom road. Small units turn left at Ligardes (signed), follow D36 for 1 km, turn right at La Romieu (signed). Otherwise continue to outskirts of Condom and take D41 left to La Romieu, through village to site.

GPS: 40.08299, 0.50183

Charges guide

Per unit incl. 2 persons and electricity	€ 17,00 - € 37,00
extra person	€ 3,60 - € 7,60
child (4-9 yrs)	no charge - € 5,40
dog (max. 2)	€ 1,50 - € 2,30

Special prices for groups, rallies, etc.

Le Camp de Florence

Route Astaffort, F-32480 La Romieu (Gers)
t: 05 62 28 15 58 e: info@lecampdeflorence.com
alanrogers.com/FR32010 www.lecampdeflorence.com

Accommodation: ✔ Pitch ✔ Mobile home/chalet ○ Hotel/B&B ○ Apartment

Camp de Florence is an attractive and very well equipped site on the edge of an historic village in pleasantly undulating Gers countryside. The 197 large, part terraced pitches (100 for tourers) all have electricity (10A), 20 with hardstanding and 16 fully serviced. They are arranged around a large field with rural views, giving a feeling of spaciousness. The 13th-century village of La Romieu is on the Santiago de Compostela pilgrims' route. The Pyrenees are a two hour drive, the Atlantic coast a similar distance. The site has been developed by the friendly Mijnsbergen family. They have sympathetically converted the old farmhouse buildings to provide facilities for the site. The Collegiate church (a UNESCO World Heritage monument) is visible from the site and well worth a visit (the views are magnificent from the top of the tower), as is the local arboretum, the biggest collection of trees in the Midi-Pyrénées.

You might like to know

Numerous walks directly from the site, from a short stroll to an all-day ramble. It is on the Santiago de Compostela pilgrims' way and it is possible to walk parts of this historical route. Mountain bike routes from site with three levels of difficulty.

- ✔ Walking notes or maps available
- ✔ Waymarked footpath – direct access from site
- ○ Waymarked footpath within 1 km. of site
- ✔ Cycle trail – direct access from site
- ○ Cycle trail access within 2 km. of site
- ✔ Mountain bike track within 2 km. of site
- ✔ Bicycle hire on site
- ○ Accompanied hiking trips
- ○ Accompanied cycling trips
- ○ Drying room for wet clothes/boots
- ✔ Packed lunch service

Facilities: One comfortable toilet block with washbasins and showers. Toilet and shower for disabled visitors. Laundry facilities. Bar with Sky TV (1/4-7/11). Restaurant and takeaway (1/7-29/8). Outdoor swimming pool (from 1/5). Fitness and games rooms. Sauna. BMX circuit. Bicycle hire. Unfenced play areas. Children's club (high season). Free WiFi. Lake fishing. Off site: Boating on the canal. Riding 10 km. Golf 15 km.

Open: 1 April - 7 November.

Directions: Turn south off N176 onto D795 signed Dol-de-Bretagne. Continue to Combourg and then take D13 to La Chapelle-aux-Filtzmeens. Continue for 2 km. to site on right.

GPS: 48.37716, -1.83705

Charges guide

Per unit incl. 2 persons and electricity	€ 23,00 - € 30,00
extra person	€ 5,00 - € 5,50
child (2-12 yrs)	€ 2,50 - € 3,00
dog	€ 2,00

France – La Chapelle-aux-Filtzmeens

Domaine du Logis

Le Logis, F-35190 La Chapelle-aux-Filtzmeens (Ille-et-Vilaine)
t: 02 99 45 25 45 e: domainedulogis@wanadoo.fr
alanrogers.com/FR35080 www.domainedulogis.com

Accommodation: ⊘ Pitch ⊘ Mobile home/chalet ○ Hotel/B&B ○ Apartment

This is an attractive rural site under new, young and enthusiastic ownership, set in the grounds of an old château. The site's upgraded modern facilities are housed in traditional converted barns and farm buildings, which are well maintained and equipped. There are a total of 188 pitches, 70 of which are for touring. The grass pitches are level, of a generous size and divided by mature hedges and trees. All have 10A electricity connections. This site would appeal to most age groups, with plenty to offer the active, including a new fitness room with a good range of modern equipment and a sauna for those who prefer to relax, or perhaps a quiet day's fishing by the lake. Although set in a quiet, rural part of the Brittany countryside, the nearby village of La Chapelle-aux-Filtzmeens has a bar, restaurant and shops. A 20 minute car ride will get you into the large town of Rennes, or perhaps travel north for 30 minutes to Mont Saint-Michel, Dinan, Dinard and the old fishing port of St Malo to sample the famous Brittany seafood.

You might like to know

The site is just 300 m. from a walking and cycling route along the Ille-et-Rance canal for discovering Rennes, Dinan or St-Malo.

- ⊘ Walking notes or maps available
- ⊘ Waymarked footpath – direct access from site
- ⊘ Waymarked footpath within 1 km. of site
- ⊘ Cycle trail – direct access from site
- ⊘ Cycle trail access within 2 km. of site
- ⊘ Mountain bike track within 2 km. of site
- ⊘ Bicycle hire on site
- ⊘ Accompanied hiking trips
- ○ Accompanied cycling trips
- ○ Drying room for wet clothes/boots
- ○ Packed lunch service

Facilities: The central well appointed sanitary block is well kept, heated in low season. Facilities for children and disabled visitors. Two smaller blocks provide facilities in high season. Busy shop. Excellent restaurant. Heated swimming pool and paddling pool (1/5-30/9; no Bermuda style shorts) with sunbathing areas. Play area. TV and games in bar. Quiet reading room. Weekly entertainment for children and adults (July/Aug) including live music. Bicycle hire (limited). WiFi. Off site: Les Abrets with shops and supermarket 2 km. Riding 6 km. Fishing 8 km. Golf 25 km.

Open: 1 April - 31 October.

Directions: Les Abrets is 70 km. southeast of Lyon at junction of D1006 (previously N6) and D1075 (previously N75). From roundabout in town take N6 towards Chambéry, turning left in just under 2 km. (signed restaurant and camping). Follow signs along country lane for just over 1 km. and entrance is on right.

GPS: 45.54115, 5.60778

Charges guide

Per unit incl. 2 persons and electricity	€ 20,00 - € 36,00
extra person	€ 4,00 - € 8,00
child (2-7 yrs)	€ 2,50 - € 5,00
dog	€ 1,50

France – Les Abrets

Kawan Village le Coin Tranquille

6 chemin des Vignes, F-38490 Les Abrets (Isère)
t: 04 76 32 13 48   e: contact@coin-tranquille.com
alanrogers.com/FR38010   www.coin-tranquille.com

Accommodation: ⊘ Pitch ⊘ Mobile home/chalet ○ Hotel/B&B ○ Apartment

Le Coin Tranquille is well placed for visits to the Savoie regions and the Alps. It is a pretty, well maintained site of 192 grass pitches (178 for tourers), all with 6A electricity. They are separated by neat hedges of hydrangea, flowering shrubs and a range of trees to make a lovely environment doubly enhanced by the rural aspect and marvellous views across to the mountains. This is a popular, family run site with friendly staff, making it a wonderful base for exploring the area. Set in the Dauphiny countryside north of Grenoble, le Coin Tranquille is truly a quiet corner, especially outside school holiday times, although it is still popular with families in high season. The Chartreuse caves near Voiron are worth visiting, as is the Monastery, and a mountain railway goes to the summit of the Chartreuse Massif.

You might like to know

An accompanied walk is organised by the site's friendly English-speaking owners every Wednesday morning in July and August.

- ⊘ Walking notes or maps available
- ⊘ Waymarked footpath – direct access from site
- ⊘ Waymarked footpath within 1 km. of site
- ○ Cycle trail – direct access from site
- ⊘ Cycle trail access within 2 km. of site
- ⊘ Mountain bike track within 2 km. of site
- ⊘ Bicycle hire on site
- ○ Accompanied hiking trips
- ○ Accompanied cycling trips
- ○ Drying room for wet clothes/boots
- ○ Packed lunch service

Facilities: Three very good toilet blocks (two very large) are colourful and very clean. Family room with facilities for babies. Excellent, spacious facilities for disabled visitors. Small launderette with ironing. Freezer space. Shop. Bar, snacks, takeaway and separate restaurant (all 18/5-15/9). Heated swimming pool (13/5-13/9). Sauna, fitness room and jacuzzi (13/5-15/9). Climbing wall. Daily activities for children (July/Aug). Guided mountain walks and other activities. Fishing. Safe hire. Barbecue area. WiFi over site (charged). Off site: Many mountain activities. Bicycle hire and riding 7 km.

Open: 13 May - 15 September.

Directions: South of Grenoble take exit 8 from A480 signed Stations de L'Oisans and follow the D1091 to Briançon. The site is signed just north of Rochetaillée at the junction with the D526. Turn here and site is immediately on the left.

GPS: 45.11530, 6.00548

Charges guide

Per unit incl. 2 persons and electricity	€ 23,20 - € 38,60
extra person	€ 5,60 - € 8,70
child (0-10 yrs)	€ 3,60 - € 5,50
dog	€ 1,00

France – Bourg-d'Oisans

Castel le Château de Rochetaillée

Chemin de Bouthean, Rochetaillée, F-38520 Bourg-d'Oisans (Isère)
t: 04 76 11 04 40 e: jcp@camping-le-chateau.com
alanrogers.com/FR38180 www.camping-le-chateau.com

Accommodation: ☑ Pitch ☑ Mobile home/chalet ☑ Hotel/B&B ○ Apartment

Set in the grounds of a small château with spectacular views, this site's ratings have recently been upgraded and it provides high quality amenities. The grounds are shared with chalets and tents to rent, with these in a separate area. There are 88 touring pitches, all with 6/10A electricity hook-ups on level areas (some large) separated by hedges and trees. The site has an excellent heated swimming pool, a fitness room, sauna, bar/restaurant and takeaway food together with a small shop selling bread and basic groceries. The site is in the centre of an area ideal for walkers, cyclists and climbers. There are good markets at Allemont (Monday) and Bourg-d'Oisans (Saturday). In high season there is a full programme of on-site activities for children, as well as excursions and activities for the whole family, including windsurfing, horse riding, hang-gliding and much more.

You might like to know

Whether you are a competitive cyclist or just enjoying a relaxing family outing, you will love Oisans, a region of glaciers, springs, lake and waterfalls, and the Ecrins National Park.

- ☑ Walking notes or maps available
- ☑ Waymarked footpath – direct access from site
- ☑ Waymarked footpath within 1 km. of site
- ○ Cycle trail – direct access from site
- ○ Cycle trail access within 2 km. of site
- ○ Mountain bike track within 2 km. of site
- ○ Bicycle hire on site
- ☑ Accompanied hiking trips
- ☑ Accompanied cycling trips
- ☑ Drying room for wet clothes/boots
- ☑ Packed lunch service

Facilities: Four toilet blocks, one heated. One block with fun facilities for children based on Disney characters. Facilities for disabled guests. Laundry facilities. Motorcaravan services. Shops, bar/restaurant, takeaway (16/4-7/9). Swimming pool complex with three pools. Water playground with inflatables. Spa, fitness centre and sauna. Play area. Games room. Sports areas. Boules. Tennis. Bicycle hire. Minigolf. Fishing. Riding. Sailing school (15/6-15/9). Communal barbecues. WiFi (charged). Free bus to beach (July-Aug). Off site: Walking and cycle ways in the forest. Atlantic beaches 5 km. Golf 10 km.

Open: 16 April - 21 September.

Directions: Site is off D652 Mimizan-Léon road, 4 km. south of crossroads with D42 at St Girons. The road to the lake and the site is signed at Vielle.

GPS: 43.90285, -1.3125

Charges guide

Per unit incl. 2 persons and electricity	€ 17,40 - € 44,60
extra person	€ 2,20 - € 7,10
child (3-12 yrs)	€ 1,70 - € 6,10
dog	€ 1,20 - € 4,50

France – Vielle-Saint-Girons

Sunêlia le Col-Vert

Lac de Léon, 1548 route de l'Etang, F-40560 Vielle-Saint-Girons (Landes)
t: 08 90 71 00 01 e: contact@colvert.com
alanrogers.com/FR40050 www.colvert.com

Accommodation: ☑ Pitch ☑ Mobile home/chalet ○ Hotel/B&B ○ Apartment

This large, well maintained campsite is well laid out on the shores of Lac de Léon and offers 185 mobile homes for rent and 380 touring pitches. The pitches range from simple ones to those with water and a drain, and there are eight with private, well designed, modern sanitary facilities. In low season it is a quiet site and those pitches beside the lake offer a wonderful backdrop to relaxing pastimes. During the main season it is a lively place for children of all ages. A pool complex offers a standard pool for swimming, a pool for children with a water canon and fountains, plenty of sunbeds and a heated indoor pool. Swimming is also permitted in the lake alongside the many water-based activities. A fitness and beauty spa offers a wide range of treatments. This extensive but natural site edges a nature reserve and stretches along the Lac de Léon, a conservation area, for 1 km. on a narrow frontage. This makes it particularly suitable for those who want to practise watersports such as sailing and windsurfing. An overall charge is made for some but not all of the leisure activities.

You might like to know

There are miles of cycle routes through the vast forests of Les Landes, including access to the region's superb beaches and typical villages.

- ☑ Walking notes or maps available
- ☑ Waymarked footpath – direct access from site
- ☑ Waymarked footpath within 1 km. of site
- ☑ Cycle trail – direct access from site
- ☑ Cycle trail access within 2 km. of site
- ☑ Mountain bike track within 2 km. of site
- ☑ Bicycle hire on site
- ☑ Accompanied hiking trips
- ☑ Accompanied cycling trips
- ○ Drying room for wet clothes/boots
- ☑ Packed lunch service

Facilities: Three modern sanitary blocks include some washbasins in cabins and baby bathrooms. Laundry facilities. Facilities for disabled visitors. Motorcaravan services. Shop. Restaurant. Takeaway in bar with terrace. Pool complex. Spa centre. 7-hectare lake (fishing, bathing, canoes, pedaloes, cable-ski). 9-hole golf course. Adventure play area. Tennis. Minigolf. Boules. Roller skating/skateboarding (bring own equipment). Bicycle hire. Internet access and WiFi (charged). Off site: Riding 6 km.

Open: 27 April - 7 September.

Directions: From A71, take Lamotte-Beuvron exit (no 3) or from N20 Orléans to Vierzon turn left on to D923 towards Aubigny. After 14 km. turn right at camping sign on to D24E. Site signed in 2 km.

GPS: 47.54398, 2.19193

Charges guide

Per unit incl. 2 persons
and electricity € 20,00 - € 46,00

extra person € 7,00 - € 10,00

child (1-17 yrs acc. to age) no charge - € 9,00

dog € 5,00 - € 7,00

Reductions for low season longer stays.

France – Pierrefitte-sur-Sauldre

Leading Camping les Alicourts

Domaine des Alicourts, F-41300 Pierrefitte-sur-Sauldre (Loir-et-Cher)
t: 02 54 88 63 34 e: info@lesalicourts.com
alanrogers.com/FR41030 www.lesalicourts.com

Accommodation: ☑ Pitch ☑ Mobile home/chalet ○ Hotel/B&B ○ Apartment

A secluded holiday village set in the heart of the forest with many sporting facilities and a super spa centre, Camping les Alicourts is midway between Orléans and Bourges, to the east of the A71. There are 490 pitches, 153 for touring and the remainder occupied by mobile homes and chalets. All pitches have electricity (6A) and good provision for water, and most are 150 sq.m. (min. 100 sq.m). Locations vary, from wooded to more open areas, thus giving a choice of amount of shade. All facilities are open all season and the leisure amenities are exceptional. The Senseo Balnéo centre offers indoor pools, hydrotherapy, massage and spa treatments for over 18s only (some special family sessions are provided). An inviting, part covered, outdoor water complex includes two swimming pools, a pool with wave machine and a beach area, not forgetting three water slides. A member of Leading Campings group.

You might like to know

The site is part of the Loire à Vélo programme.

☑ Walking notes or maps available
○ Waymarked footpath – direct access from site
☑ Waymarked footpath within 1 km. of site
○ Cycle trail – direct access from site
○ Cycle trail access within 2 km. of site
☑ Mountain bike track within 2 km. of site
☑ Bicycle hire on site
○ Accompanied hiking trips
○ Accompanied cycling trips
○ Drying room for wet clothes/boots
☑ Packed lunch service

Facilities: The main toilet block is well maintained, if a little dated, and is well equipped including washbasins in cabins, provision for disabled visitors, and a baby bathroom. Laundry facilities. Shop. Bar and small restaurant with takeaway (1/5-15/9). Covered and heated swimming pool (at 28 degrees when we visited) and paddling pool (all season). Play area. TV. Entertainment in season including miniclub. Fishing and pedalos on the lake. Torches useful. WiFi (charged). Off site: Golf 7 km. Riding 10 km. Beach 20 km.

Open: 1 May - 30 September.

Directions: Site is signed from D33 Pontchâteau-Herbignac road near Ste Reine. Also signed from the D773 and N165-E60 (exit 13).

GPS: 47.44106, -2.15981

Charges guide

Per unit incl. 2 persons
and electricity € 19,08 - € 27,91

extra person	€ 3,43 - € 5,74
child (2-12 yrs)	€ 2,42 - € 4,11

Kawan Village du Deffay

B.P. 18 Le Deffay, Sainte Reine-de-Bretagne, F-44160 Pontchâteau (Loire-Atlantique)
t: 02 40 88 00 57   e: campingdudeffay@wanadoo.fr
alanrogers.com/FR44090   www.camping-le-deffay.com

Accommodation: ☑ Pitch   ☑ Mobile home/chalet   ☑ Hotel/B&B   ○ Apartment

A family managed site, Château du Deffay is a refreshing departure from the usual formula in that it is not over organised or supervised and has no tour operator units. The 170 good sized, fairly level pitches have pleasant views and are either on open grass, on shallow terraces divided by hedges, or informally arranged in a central, slightly sloping wooded area. Most have electricity (6/10A). The bar, restaurant and covered pool are located within the old courtyard area of the smaller château that dates from before 1400. A significant attraction of the site is the large, unfenced lake which is well stocked for fishermen and even has free pedaloes for children. The landscape is wonderfully natural and the site blends well with the rural environment of the estate, lake and farmland which surround it. Alpine type chalets overlook the lake and fit in well with the environment and the larger château (built in 1880 and now offering B&B) stands slightly away from the camping area but provides a wonderful backdrop for an evening stroll.

You might like to know

Why not take part in one of the themed treks (nature, trees etc) through the beautiful local countryside?

☑ Walking notes or maps available
☑ Waymarked footpath – direct access from site
☑ Waymarked footpath within 1 km. of site
○ Cycle trail – direct access from site
○ Cycle trail access within 2 km. of site
○ Mountain bike track within 2 km. of site
☑ Bicycle hire on site
○ Accompanied hiking trips
○ Accompanied cycling trips
○ Drying room for wet clothes/boots
○ Packed lunch service

Kawan Village les Bois du Bardelet

Route de Bourges, le Petit Bardelet, F-45500 Gien (Loiret)
t: 02 38 67 47 39 e: contact@bardelet.com
alanrogers.com/FR45010 www.bardelet.com

Accommodation: ☑ Pitch ☑ Mobile home/chalet ○ Hotel/B&B ○ Apartment

This attractive, high quality site, ideal for families with young children, is in a rural setting and well situated for exploring the less well known eastern part of the Loire Valley. Two lakes (one for boating, one for fishing) and a pool complex have been attractively landscaped in 18 hectares of former farmland, blending old and new with natural wooded areas and more open grassland with rural views. There are 245 large, level grass pitches with 120 for touring units. All have at least 10A electricity, 15 have water, waste water and 16A electricity, and some 30 have hardstanding. Eight have individual en-suite sanitary units beside the pitch. Attractively converted former farm buildings house a bar with a pleasant terrace and an excellent restaurant with a covered terrace overlooking a small lake. There is an impressive range of leisure facilities including an indoor pool with jacuzzi, a new wellness suite with hot tub and sauna, and a delightful and imaginative heated indoor water play area for children. A family club card can be purchased (€5/day) to make use of any of the charged activities.

You might like to know

Just 5 km. from the River Loire, the site is part of the Loire à Vélo programme. The knowledgeable and friendly team in reception will be pleased to help you make the most of the Loire Valley by bicycle.

- ☑ Walking notes or maps available
- ○ Waymarked footpath – direct access from site
- ○ Waymarked footpath within 1 km. of site
- ○ Cycle trail – direct access from site
- ☑ Cycle trail access within 2 km. of site
- ○ Mountain bike track within 2 km. of site
- ☑ Bicycle hire on site
- ○ Accompanied hiking trips
- ○ Accompanied cycling trips
- ○ Drying room for wet clothes/boots
- ○ Packed lunch service

Facilities: Two heated toilet blocks (effectively unisex, one open in high season only) have some washbasins in cubicles, controllable showers, an en-suite unit for disabled visitors and a baby room. Washing machines and dryers. Minimart, bar, takeaway and restaurant (all 1/5-15/9). Heated outdoor pool (1/5-31/8). Heated indoor pool and children's pool. Wellness centre with sauna, hot tub, Shiatsu massage and beauty treatments. Fitness and jacuzzi rooms. Beach on lake. Games area. Canoeing and fishing. Tennis. Minigolf. Volleyball. Pétanque. Children's playground with trampoline. Kids' club, sports tournaments, excursions and activities, aquagym, archery (July/Aug). Bicycle hire. Chalets/mobile homes for hire. Free WiFi in bar area. Off site: Supermarket 5 km. Shops, bars, restaurants, museums and Wednesday market 6 km. Riding 6 km. Boat launching 12 km. Sailing and golf 25 km. Walking and cycling routes.

Open: 19 April - 30 September.

Directions: Gien is 60 km. southeast of Orléans. Site is 7 km. south of Gien. Leave A77 autoroute at exit 19 and take D940 (Bourges) to bypass Gien. Continue on D940 for 5 km. At junction with D53 (no left turn) turn right and right again to cross D940. Follow signs for 1.5 km. to site.

GPS: 47.64152, 2.61528

Charges guide

Per unit incl. 2 persons and electricity	€ 20,10 - € 33,50
extra person (over 2 yrs)	€ 5,20 - € 6,90
dog	€ 4,00

Facilities: First class toilet blocks. Facilities for disabled visitors and babies. Washing machine and airers (no lines allowed). Motorcaravan services. Bar, small shop and takeaway (1/5-15/9). Lounge, library, TV, upstairs games/reading room. Bird watching is a speciality of the site and equipment is available. Infrared sauna and jacuzzi. Music room. Play area for the very young. Small beach beside river. Boules. Giant chess. Weekly evening meal in May, June and Sept. Internet. Walks organised. WiFi over site (free in bar). Off site: Village with two restaurants. Bicycle hire and riding 4 km. Walking and hiking.

Open: 29 March - 20 October.

Directions: At Argelès-Gazost, take D918 towards Aucun. After 8 km. turn left on D13 to Bun, cross the river, then right on D103 to site (5.5 km). Narrow road, few passing places.

GPS: 42.94152, -0.17726

Charges guide

Per unit incl. 2 persons and electricity	€ 19,00 - € 44,50
extra person	€ 5,85 - € 42,00
child (under 8 yrs)	€ 3,80
dog	€ 3,00

France – Estaing

Camping Pyrénées Natura

Route du Lac, F-65400 Estaing (Hautes-Pyrénées)
t: 05 62 97 45 44 e: info@camping-pyrenees-natura.com
alanrogers.com/FR65060 www.camping-pyrenees-natura.com

Accommodation: ☑ Pitch ☑ Mobile home/chalet ○ Hotel/B&B ○ Apartment

Pyrénées Natura, at an altitude of 1,000 m. on the edge of the national park, is the perfect site for lovers of nature. The 66 pitches (47 for tourers), all with electricity (3-10A), are in a landscaped area with 75 varieties of trees and shrubs – but they do not spoil the fantastic views. A traditional-style building houses the reception, bar and indoor games/reading room. There is a small, well stocked shop in the former watermill. Prices are very reasonable and homemade bread can be purchased. On the river there is a small beach belonging to the site for supervised water play. The owners, the Papin family, will do all they can to make your stay a pleasant one. Their aim is that you return home feeling at peace with the world and having learnt something about the area and its flora and fauna, especially the birds which soar above the site. There are several unusual hens on site and you are encouraged to use the free birdspotting telescope!

You might like to know

Virginia and Hervé will help arrange a tailor-made holiday in the heart of the Pyrenees. After negotiating the famous passes of Tourmalet, Aubisque, Hautacam and Soulor, relax and unwind with a sauna and jacuzzi.

☑ Walking notes or maps available
☑ Waymarked footpath – direct access from site
☑ Waymarked footpath within 1 km. of site
○ Cycle trail – direct access from site
○ Cycle trail access within 2 km. of site
○ Mountain bike track within 2 km. of site
○ Bicycle hire on site
☑ Accompanied hiking trips
○ Accompanied cycling trips
○ Drying room for wet clothes/boots
☑ Packed lunch service

Camping Soleil du Pibeste

16 avenue du Lavedan, F-65400 Agos-Vidalos (Hautes-Pyrénées)
t: 06 72 32 17 04 e: info@campingpibeste.com
alanrogers.com/FR65090 www.campingpibeste.com

Accommodation: ☑ Pitch ☑ Mobile home/chalet ○ Hotel/B&B ○ Apartment

Facilities: Two heated toilet blocks. Facilities for disabled visitors. Baby room. Cleaning can be variable. Washing machine, dryer. Motorcaravan services. Bar, snack bar, restaurant and pizzeria (June-Sept). Shop for essentials. Bread can be ordered for next day delivery. Swimming pool with panoramic views and loungers (opening dates vary with weather). New children's play areas (4-6 yrs and 6-10 yrs). Multisports pitch. Volleyball. Tennis. Badminton. Bowling. Basketball. 4 free activities weekly (tai chi, qi gong, rollerblading, archery, etc; July/Aug). Entertainment programme, children's activities and craft workshops (July/Aug). Massage (charged). Library. Free WiFi over site. Off site: Fishing 800 m. Rafting 2 km. Golf 10 km. Riding 15 km. Skiing 20 km.

Open: 1 May - 30 October.

Directions: Agos Vidalos is on the N21, which becomes the D821, 5 km. south of Lourdes. Leave expressway at second exit, signed Agos Vidalos and continue on D921B to site, a short distance on the right.

GPS: 43.03557, -0.07093

Charges guide

Per unit incl. 2 persons and electricity	€ 26,00 - € 37,00
extra person	€ 8,00
dog	€ 5,00

The Dusserm family, the owners, are very proud of their regional culture and heritage and will ensure you are made welcome. The reception is friendly, with an area for local foods, maps and good tourist information. This site is special because of the range and type of activities that it offers. These include tai chi, qi gong, massage, archery, walking, climbing and canoeing. Choral and creative activities are offered. There are 40 touring pitches all with 6-10A electricity. Mobile homes and chalets are available to rent. The mountain view from the terrace is magnificent. Ongoing improvements include a dedicated motorcaravan parking area. Play areas have been expanded to cater for different age groups, including lively teenagers. There is a shop and bread can be ordered for delivery the following morning. The site is rural but has a bus stop just outside providing access to Argelès-Gazost and the renowned pilgrimage town of Lourdes. The family also offers a pick up service from various airports and towns, and car hire.

You might like to know

The friendly campsite owners know the Pyrenees very well and organise accompanied walks for all abilities.

☑ Walking notes or maps available
○ Waymarked footpath – direct access from site
☑ Waymarked footpath within 1 km. of site
○ Cycle trail – direct access from site
☑ Cycle trail access within 2 km. of site
○ Mountain bike track within 2 km. of site
○ Bicycle hire on site
☑ Accompanied hiking trips
○ Accompanied cycling trips
○ Drying room for wet clothes/boots
○ Packed lunch service

Facilities: Two bright, modern sanitary blocks provide showers and washbasins in cubicles. Baby bath and changing. En-suite facility for disabled visitors. Laundry. Motorcaravan services arranged. Shop (fresh food in high season), bar/restaurant and takeaway (all season). Outdoor pool with paddling pool and flume (15/6-15/9), terrace and loungers. Indoor heated pool (15/4-15/9). Solarium. Fitness room. Play area. Free fishing on small lake (fenced and gated). Children's club, daytime activities and evening entertainment (July/Aug). Games area (with TV projected onto large screen for major events). TV in side room. Volleyball. Go-karts. Children's cycle circuit. Bicycle hire. Internet point. WiFi (charged) in bar area. Off site: Riding 4 km. Beach and sailing 7 km. Golf 8 km. St Jean-de-Monts 8 km. Saint Hilaire-de-Riez 10 km.

Open: 1 April - 2 October.

Directions: Le Perrier is 51 km. northwest of La Roche-sur-Yon and 11 km. southwest of Challans. Site is 2 km. to south on D59 to Le Pissot and St Gilles; from the new route of the D205 Challans-St Jean-de-Monts road turn south on D59 and site is on right in 300 m.

GPS: 46.80133, -1.980656

Charges guide

Per unit incl. 2 persons and electricity	€ 18,00 - € 33,00
extra person	€ 5,00 - € 7,50
child (2-11 yrs)	€ 3,00 - € 6,30
dog (max. 2)	€ 3,00 - € 3,50

Domaine le Jardin du Marais

208 route de Saint-Gilles, F-85300 Le Perrier (Vendée)
t: **02 51 68 09 17**   e: info@lejardindumarais.eu
alanrogers.com/FR85635   www.campsite-nature.co.uk/

Accommodation: ✔ Pitch   ✔ Mobile home/chalet   ○ Hotel/B&B   ○ Apartment

Le Perrier is a small village in the heart of the marshes, characterised by the flat land and vast prairies surrounding it. Le Jardin du Marais is a delightful, family site in a country setting on the edge of the marshes. It is beautifully kept and has excellent facilities including a well stocked shop, a pleasant bar/restaurant and a good pool complex. The enthusiastic and hardworking owners are keen to welcome more British visitors who will be sure of a warm reception. Of the 120 pitches, 50 are available for touring: the established pitches offer some shade and have electricity and water nearby; a new area offers large pitches with electricity, water and drainage. The beaches are just seven kilometres away. For shops, bars and restaurants you can use the nearby village of Le Perrier or head for the resorts of Saint Jean-de-Monts or Saint Hilaire-de-Riez where there are also large supermarkets and frequent markets. Just south of Saint Hilaire is the busy fishing port and resort of Saint Gilles Croix-de-Vie. A Sites et Paysages member.

You might like to know

St Jean-de-Monts has recently opened an excellent 26 km. cycle track which runs close to the coast.

- ✔ Walking notes or maps available
- ○ Waymarked footpath – direct access from site
- ✔ Waymarked footpath within 1 km. of site
- ○ Cycle trail – direct access from site
- ✔ Cycle trail access within 2 km. of site
- ○ Mountain bike track within 2 km. of site
- ✔ Bicycle hire on site
- ○ Accompanied hiking trips
- ○ Accompanied cycling trips
- ○ Drying room for wet clothes/boots
- ○ Packed lunch service

United Kingdom – Bodmin

South Penquite Farm

South Penquite, Blisland, Bodmin PL30 4LH (Cornwall)
t: 01208 850491   e: thefarm@bodminmoor.co.uk
alanrogers.com/UK0302   www.southpenquite.co.uk

Accommodation: ☑ Pitch   ☑ Mobile home/chalet   ○ Hotel/B&B   ○ Apartment

South Penquite offers real camping with no frills. It is set on a 200-hectare hill farm, high on Bodmin Moor between the villages of Blisland and St Breward. The farm achieved organic status in 2001 and runs a flock of 100 ewes and a herd of 20 cattle and horses. The camping is small scale and intended to have a low impact on the surrounding environment. Fifty tents or simple motorcaravans (no caravans) can pitch around the edge of three walled fields, roughly cut in the midst of the moor. You can find shelter or a view. Four yurts are available to rent in one field, complete with wood burning stoves. Campfires are permitted with wood available from the farmhouse. You will also find horses, ponies, chickens, geese, ducks and turkeys. A walk of some two miles takes you over most of the farm and some of the moor, taking in a Bronze Age hut settlement, the river and a standing stone. It is also possible to fish for brown trout on the farm's stretch of the De Lank river.

You might like to know

South Penquite Farm runs a number of bushcraft days during the summer holidays. These family days are an introduction to bushcraft and nature awareness skills, learning about the local wildlife and the environment in a fun and engaging way.

- ☑ Walking notes or maps available
- ☑ Waymarked footpath – direct access from site
- ○ Waymarked footpath within 1 km. of site
- ○ Cycle trail – direct access from site
- ☑ Cycle trail access within 2 km. of site
- ○ Mountain bike track within 2 km. of site
- ○ Bicycle hire on site
- ○ Accompanied hiking trips
- ○ Accompanied cycling trips
- ○ Drying room for wet clothes/boots
- ○ Packed lunch service

Facilities: A smart new pine clad toilet block, with a separate provision of four family-sized showers, with solar heated rainwater. Washing machine and dryer. Small fridge and freezer. Home produced lamb, burgers and sausages available. Facilities for field studies and opportunities for educational groups and schools to learn about the local environment. Bushcraft days. Arts workshops. Fishing (requires an EA rod licence and tokens available from the West Country Rivers Trust). Dogs are not accepted. Off site: Riding and cycling 1 mile. Pubs 1.5 and 2.5 miles. Sustrans Route 3 passes close by. North and south coasts within easy reach.

Open: 1 April - 31 October.

Directions: On A30 Bodmin Moor pass Jamaica Inn and sign for Colliford Lake and watch for St Breward sign (to right) immediately at end of dual carriageway. Follow narrow road over moor for 2 miles ignoring any turns, including right turn to St Breward just before South Penquite sign. Follow track over stone bridge through farm gate, then bear left to camping fields. Book in at Farm House.
GPS: 50.54221, -4.67144

Charges guide

Per person	£ 8,00
child (5-15 yrs)	£ 4,00

Less 10% for stays of 5 nights or more. No credit cards.

Facilities: Five identical toilet blocks, each looked after by resident wardens, are fully equipped and provide good, functional facilities, each block with laundry facilities. The newest block (in field 5) has under-floor heating and includes facilities for disabled visitors. Extra good facilities for disabled visitors and private family washrooms are beside reception. Well stocked shop. Good value takeaway with restaurant area. Bars and entertainment in season. Indoor pool (22x10 m; heated Easter-Oct) at a small charge. Riding. 18-hole pitch and putt. Crazy golf. 'Kiddies kar' track (all charged). Games room. Large play area. Games and activities organised in high season. WiFi. ATM. Woodland walks. Max. 2 dogs (in separate areas). Summer parking and winter caravan storage. Caravan sales, workshop, accessories and repair centre. Rallies accepted. Off site: Fishing and boat launching 4 miles. Bicycle hire 10 miles.

Open: All year.

Directions: From Barnstaple take A39 towards Lynton. After 1 mile turn left on B3230. Turn right at garage on A3123 and park is 1.5 miles on the right.

GPS: 51.174983, -4.05475

Charges guide

Per unit incl. 2 persons and electricity	£ 8,90 - £ 25,70
extra person	no charge - £ 4,50
child (5-12 yrs)	no charge - £ 2,50
dog	£ 1,70 - £ 2,70

Low and mid season discounts for over 50s.

Stowford Farm Meadows

Berry Down, Combe Martin, Ilfracombe EX34 0PW (Devon)
t: 01271 882476   e: enquiries@stowford.co.uk
alanrogers.com/UK0690   www.stowford.co.uk

Accommodation: ☑ Pitch   ☑ Mobile home/chalet   ○ Hotel/B&B   ○ Apartment

Stowford Farm is a friendly, family park set in 500 acres of the rolling North Devon countryside, available for recreation and walking, yet within easy reach of five local beaches. The touring park and its facilities have been developed in the fields and farm buildings surrounding the old farmhouse and provide a village like centre with a comfortable, spacious feel. There are 710 pitches on five slightly sloping meadows separated by hedges. The numbered and marked pitches, some with hardstanding, are accessed by hard roads, most have 10/16A electricity and there are well placed water points. Stowford also provides plenty to keep the whole family occupied without leaving the park, including woodland walks and horse riding from the park's own stables. There is entertainment in high season including barn dances, discos, karaoke and other musical evenings. There is also much for children to do including an under-cover mini zoo where they can handle many sorts of animals (on payment).

You might like to know

Seventy acres of woodland has been left for site users' enjoyment and education and provides an excellent network of waymarked paths and tracks leading deep into the beautiful wooded Bittadon Valley.

- ☑ Walking notes or maps available
- ☑ Waymarked footpath – direct access from site
- ○ Waymarked footpath within 1 km. of site
- ○ Cycle trail – direct access from site
- ☑ Cycle trail access within 2 km. of site
- ○ Mountain bike track within 2 km. of site
- ○ Bicycle hire on site
- ○ Accompanied hiking trips
- ○ Accompanied cycling trips
- ○ Drying room for wet clothes/boots
- ○ Packed lunch service

Facilities: The purpose built, heated toilet block (refurbished in 2010) is of a high standard including an excellent bathroom for disabled visitors, although the showers are rather compact. Baby room. Laundry. Motorcaravan service point. Play area. Field for ball games. Bicycle hire. Beauty treatments. WiFi throughout (charged). Off site: Golf and riding 0.5 miles. Beach 1.5 miles. Fishing 4 miles. Martin Mere nature reserve nearby.

Open: All year excl. February.

Directions: Park is 4 miles south of Southport. From Ainsdale on A565 travel south for 1.5 miles to second traffic lights (Woodvale) and turn right into Coastal Road to site on left in 150 yds. From south pass RAF Woodvale and turn left at second set of lights.

GPS: 53.5888, -3.044

Charges guide

Per unit incl. 2 persons and electricity	£ 14,50 - £ 17,70
hardstanding	£ 1,70
extra person	£ 3,50
child (5-16 yrs)	£ 2,55
dog (max. 2)	£ 1,35

Willowbank Holiday Home & Touring Park

Coastal Road, Ainsdale, Southport PR8 3ST (Mersey)
t: 01704 571566 e: info@willowbankcp.co.uk
alanrogers.com/UK5360 www.willowbankcp.co.uk

Accommodation: ☑ Pitch ○ Mobile home/chalet ○ Hotel/B&B ○ Apartment

Willowbank Park is well situated for the Sefton coast and Southport, set on the edge of sand dunes amongst mature, wind swept trees. Entrance to the park is controlled by a barrier, with a pass-key issued at the excellent reception building which doubles as a sales office for the substantial, high quality caravan holiday home development. There are 87 touring pitches, 30 on gravel hardstandings, 24 on grass and a further 33 pitches, all with 16A electricity; these are on grass hardstanding using an environmentally friendly reinforcement system. Large units are accepted by prior arrangement. The owners are very well supported by the reception team which has considerable experience in managing the touring park. There could be some noise from the nearby main road. This is a good area for cycling and walking with the Trans Pennine Way being adjacent. The area is famous for its golf courses including the Royal Birkdale championship links. Latest arrival time is 21.00.

You might like to know

For cyclists of all ages it is easy to get around on the many cycle routes covering the area, and there is good access to the Trans-Pennine Trail located just off the park. Bicycles are available for hire.

- ☑ Walking notes or maps available
- ☑ Waymarked footpath – direct access from site
- ☑ Waymarked footpath within 1 km. of site
- ☑ Cycle trail – direct access from site
- ☑ Cycle trail access within 2 km. of site
- ○ Mountain bike track within 2 km. of site
- ☑ Bicycle hire on site
- ○ Accompanied hiking trips
- ○ Accompanied cycling trips
- ○ Drying room for wet clothes/boots
- ○ Packed lunch service

Castlerigg Hall Caravan & Camping Park

Castlerigg Hall, Keswick CA12 4TE (Cumbria)
t: 01768 774499 e: info@castlerigg.co.uk
alanrogers.com/UK5660 www.castlerigg.co.uk

Accommodation: ☑ Pitch ☑ Mobile home/chalet ○ Hotel/B&B ○ Apartment

This well laid out park was started in the late 1950s by the Jackson family, who over the years have developed and improved the site whilst maintaining its character. Traditional stone buildings house the reception and shop. A modern amenity block includes an excellent campers' kitchen. Tarmac roads wend their way around the site to the separate tent area of 110 pitches. Gently sloping with some shelter, these pitches have fine views across Keswick, Derwentwater and the western Fells. The 45 caravan pitches tend to be on terraces, again overlooking the lake. Each terrace has a maximum of eight pitches, all on hardstanding and with 10A electricity and nearly all with a water tap and grey water drain. Places to visit include Keswick (about 20 minutes walk), Derwentwater, Ullswater, Penrith, Carlisle, Hadrian's Wall and, quite close to the site, Castlerigg stone circle which is believed to be some 4,000 years old, and of course as much walking as you might want.

You might like to know

The park is only a 45 minute walk from the summit of Walla Crag, regarded as one of the best viewpoints in England. Whinlatter Forest cycle trails are accessible by a bike bus, with various grades of trail available. The Castlerigg Gallery displays stunning landscape photography of the local area.

- ☑ Walking notes or maps available
- ☑ Waymarked footpath – direct access from site
- ☑ Waymarked footpath within 1 km. of site
- ○ Cycle trail – direct access from site
- ☑ Cycle trail access within 2 km. of site
- ☑ Mountain bike track within 2 km. of site
- ○ Bicycle hire on site
- ○ Accompanied hiking trips
- ○ Accompanied cycling trips
- ☑ Drying room for wet clothes/boots
- ○ Packed lunch service

Facilities: The main toilet block is beautifully fitted out, fully tiled and heated, with showers, vanity style washbasins (2 in cabins) and hair care areas. Unit for disabled visitors (key). Baby area. Fully equipped laundry and dishwashing area. Games room and campers' kitchen complete with microwave, toasters, kettle and hot plates. Two other toilet blocks are older in style but newly decorated and clean. Reception houses tourist information and a well stocked shop (with gas). WiFi over part of site. Restaurant with locally sourced food. Arts and craft gallery. Off site: Hotel/pub for meals adjacent to site. Fishing, golf, riding, bicycle hire and boat launching, all 2 km.

Open: 12 March - 7 November.

Directions: From Penrith take A66 towards Keswick and Cockermouth. Leave at first sign for Keswick (A591) and follow to junction (A5271). Turn left on A591 signed Windermere and after 1 mile, take small road on right signed Castlerigg and Rakefoot. Park entrance is on right after 400 yds.

GPS: 54.5931, -3.112583

Charges guide

Per unit incl. 2 persons and electricity	£ 19,50 - £ 29,00
extra person (over 4 yrs)	£ 3,50 - £ 5,00
tent per adult	£ 6,95 - £ 8,90
dog	£ 1,60 - £ 2,40

Pen-y-Bont Touring & Camping Park

Llangynog Road, Bala LL23 7PH (Gwynedd)
t: 01678 520549 e: penybont-bala@btconnect.co.uk
alanrogers.com/UK6340 www.penybont-bala.co.uk

Accommodation: ☑ Pitch ☑ Mobile home/chalet ○ Hotel/B&B ○ Apartment

This is a pretty little park with 59 touring pitches, 47 of which have hardstanding. Connected by circular gravel roads, they are intermingled with trees and tall trees edge the site. Electricity connections (16A) are available, including 11 for tents, and there are 28 serviced pitches with hardstanding, electricity, water and drainage. There are also pitches for 25 seasonal units. The park entrance and the stone building that houses reception and the well stocked shop provide quite a smart image. With views of the Berwyn mountains, Pen-y-bont has a peaceful, attractive and useful location being the closest park to Bala town. Bala Lake is 100 yards and the park is three miles from the Welsh National White Water Centre, with Snowdonia on hand.

You might like to know

There is an excellent walk from the site, leading above Bala to get a great view of Wales' largest natural lake.

- ☑ Walking notes or maps available
- ☑ Waymarked footpath – direct access from site
- ○ Waymarked footpath within 1 km. of site
- ○ Cycle trail – direct access from site
- ☑ Cycle trail access within 2 km. of site
- ☑ Mountain bike track within 2 km. of site
- ○ Bicycle hire on site
- ○ Accompanied hiking trips
- ○ Accompanied cycling trips
- ○ Drying room for wet clothes/boots
- ○ Packed lunch service

Facilities: The toilet block includes washbasins in cubicles and spacious hot showers. Two new cubicles with washbasin and WC. Separate laundry room and an en-suite unit for disabled visitors that doubles as a baby room, operated by key (£5 deposit). Outside covered area with fencing and concrete floor for dishwashing sinks and bins. Motorcaravan service point. Shop. Bicycle hire arranged. Caravan storage. WiFi (charged). 2 Romany-style caravans for rent. Off site: Fishing 200 yds. Boat launching, golf and riding 2 miles. Mon. market in Bala.

Open: 15 March - 27 October.

Directions: Park is 0.5 miles southeast of Bala village on the B4391. Bala is between Dolgellau and Corwen on the A494.

GPS: 52.901717, -3.590117

Charges guide

Per unit incl. 2 persons and electricity	£ 19,00 - £ 23,00
tent pitch incl. 2 persons	£ 15,50 - £ 20,50
extra person	£ 7,50
child (4-16 yrs)	£ 4,00
dog	£ 1,00

Hoddom Castle Caravan Park

Hoddom, Lockerbie DG11 1AS (Dumfries and Galloway)
t: 01576 300251   e: hoddomcastle@aol.com
alanrogers.com/UK6910   www.hoddomcastle.co.uk

Accommodation: ☑ Pitch   ☑ Mobile home/chalet   ◯ Hotel/B&B   ◯ Apartment

Facilities: The main toilet block can be heated and is very well appointed. Washbasins in cubicles, three en-suite cubicles with WC and basin (one with baby facilities) and an en-suite shower unit for disabled visitors. Two further tiled blocks, kept very clean, provide washbasins and WCs only. Well equipped laundry room at the castle. Motorcaravan service point. Licensed shop at reception (gas available). Bar, restaurant and takeaway (Easter-Oct). Games room. Large, grass play area. Crazy golf. Mountain bike trail. Fishing. Golf. Guided walks (high season). WiFi in bar. Caravan storage. Off site: Tennis nearby. Riding 3 miles. Beach 6 miles. Boat launching and sailing 10 miles.

Open: 1 April - 30 October.

Directions: Leave A74M at exit 19 (Ecclefechan) and follow signs to park. Leave A75 at Annan junction (west end of Annan bypass) and follow signs.

GPS: 55.041367, -3.311

Charges guide

Per unit incl. 2 persons
and electricity £ 15,50 - £ 22,50

extra person £ 3,00

The park around Hoddom Castle is landscaped, spacious and well laid out on mainly sloping ground with many mature and beautiful trees, originally part of an arboretum. The drive to the site is just under a mile long with a one way system. Many of the 91 numbered touring pitches have good views of the castle and have gravel hardstanding with grass for awnings. Most have 16A electrical connections. In front of the castle are flat fields used for tents and caravans with a limited number of electricity hook-ups. The oldest part of Hoddom Castle itself is a 16th-century Borders Pele Tower, or fortified Keep. This was extended to form a residence for a Lancashire cotton magnate, became a youth hostel and was then taken over by the army during WW2. Since then parts have been demolished but the original Border Keep still survives, unfortunately in a semi-derelict state. The park's nine-hole golf course is in an attractive setting alongside the Annan river, where fishing is possible for salmon and trout. Coarse fishing is also possible elsewhere on the estate.

You might like to know

In the woods surrounding the site there is a mountain bike trail on which anyone can test their off-road skills. The track is about half a mile long and twists and turns through thick bushes and trees.

- ☑ Walking notes or maps available
- ◯ Waymarked footpath – direct access from site
- ☑ Waymarked footpath within 1 km. of site
- ◯ Cycle trail – direct access from site
- ☑ Cycle trail access within 2 km. of site
- ☑ Mountain bike track within 2 km. of site
- ◯ Bicycle hire on site
- ◯ Accompanied hiking trips
- ◯ Accompanied cycling trips
- ◯ Drying room for wet clothes/boots
- ◯ Packed lunch service

Loch Ken Holiday Park

Parton, Castle Douglas DG7 3NE (Dumfries and Galloway)
t: 01644 470282 e: office@lochkenholidaypark.co.uk
alanrogers.com/UK6940 www.lochkenholidaypark.co.uk

Accommodation: ☑ Pitch ☑ Mobile home/chalet ○ Hotel/B&B ○ Apartment

Loch Ken Holiday Park sits right on the shore of the loch, adjacent to the RSPB bird reserve and the Galloway Forest Park – it is a peaceful haven in an Area of Outstanding Natural Beauty. This is a family owned park with 40 touring pitches and 33 caravan holiday homes, ten of which are for rent. The touring pitches, all with 10A electricity, are quite separate and are arranged in a mostly open plan way on a large, neatly mown grass area beside the water. Some of this area is gently undulating. Mature trees border the park and provide an area for walking dogs. Site lighting is minimal so torches are advised. The spacious reception and well stocked shop are centrally located with a separate, well presented tourist information area. There are facilities for launching small boats, but these must be registered with the local council (at reception). This park is probably mostly suited to couples and families with older children who enjoy outdoor pursuits.

Facilities: The toilet block has been completely refurbished to modern standards and was exceptionally clean when we visited. Separate facilities in a modern Portacabin unit are provided in the tent area. Facilities for disabled visitors. Gas supplies. Well stocked shop. Good play area. Bicycles, canoes and dinghies for hire. Boat launching (permit from reception). Fishing (permit). Off site: Buses stop at the entrance, but are limited. Skiing 0.5 miles. Golf and riding 7 miles. Bars and restaurants in Castle Douglas 9 miles. Kirkcudbright 15 miles.

Open: 1 March - 31 October.

Directions: From Castle Douglas take the A713 north for 7 miles. Site entrance is on left in Parton.
GPS: 55.0104, -4.05568

Charges guide

Per unit incl. 2 persons, 2 children and electricity	£ 17,00 - £ 22,00
tent, no electricity	£ 12,00 - £ 17,00
extra person	£ 2,00
dog	£ 2,00

You might like to know

The 7 Stanes are seven mountain biking trail centres spanning the south of Scotland, most within easy access of the site, and offering some of the country's best mountain biking.

- ☑ Walking notes or maps available
- ○ Waymarked footpath – direct access from site
- ○ Waymarked footpath within 1 km. of site
- ○ Cycle trail – direct access from site
- ○ Cycle trail access within 2 km. of site
- ○ Mountain bike track within 2 km. of site
- ☑ Bicycle hire on site
- ○ Accompanied hiking trips
- ○ Accompanied cycling trips
- ○ Drying room for wet clothes/boots
- ○ Packed lunch service

Facilities:
Facilities: The large, well maintained main toilet block includes 10 unisex cabins with shower, basin and WC, and 12 with washbasin and WC. A second, excellent block next to the tent areas has en-suite shower rooms (one for disabled visitors) and bathroom, separate washing cubicles, showers and baby room. Laundry facilities. Motorcaravan service point. Gas supplies. Licensed shop. Bar, restaurant and takeaway (all year). Golf and Leisure Club with indoor pool (all year). Play area (incl. toddlers' area). Pony trekking. Quad bikes, boating pond, 10-pin bowling, playgrounds, putting. Nature trails. Coarse fishing ponds plus sea angling and an all-tide slipway for boating enthusiasts. Caravan storage. WiFi over site, free in bistro. Purpose built chalet for tourist information and leisure facility bookings. Off site: Small sandy beach nearby.

Open: All year.

Directions: In Kirkcudbright turn onto A755 and cross river bridge. In 400 yds. turn left onto B727 at international camping sign. Or follow Brighouse Bay signs off A75 just east of Gatehouse of Fleet.

GPS: 54.7875, -4.1291

Charges guide

Per unit incl. 2 persons and electricity	£ 19,50 - £ 26,00
extra person	£ 3,00
child (5-15 yrs)	£ 2,00
dog	£ 2,00

Contact park for full charges. Golf packages in low season.

Brighouse Bay Holiday Park

Brighouse Bay, Borgue, Kirkcudbright DG6 4TS (Dumfries and Galloway)
t: 01557 870267   e: info@gillespie-leisure.co.uk
alanrogers.com/UK6950   www.brighouse-bay.co.uk

Accommodation: ☑ Pitch   ☑ Mobile home/chalet   ○ Hotel/B&B   ☑ Apartment

Hidden away within 1,200 exclusive acres, on a quiet, unspoilt peninsula, this spacious family park is only some 200 yards through bluebell woods from an open, sandy bay. Over 90 percent of the 210 touring caravan pitches have 10/16A electricity, some with hardstanding and some with water, drainage and TV aerial. The three tent areas are on fairly flat, undulating ground and some pitches have electricity. There are 120 self-contained holiday caravans and lodges of which about 30 are let, the rest privately owned. On-site leisure facilities include a golf and leisure club with 16.5 m. pool, water features, jacuzzi, steam room, fitness room, games room (all on payment), golf driving range, bowling green and clubhouse bar and bistro. The 18-hole golf course extends onto the headland with superb views. A nine-hole family golf course is popular. The TRSS Approved Pony Trekking Centre offers treks for complete beginners and a range of hacks for the more experienced. This is a well run park of high standards and a member of the Best of British group.

You might like to know

The Southern Upland Way is Scotland's longest walk, stretching 212 miles between Portpatrick and Cocksburnpath, and is easily accessed from the site.

- ☑ Walking notes or maps available
- ○ Waymarked footpath – direct access from site
- ☑ Waymarked footpath within 1 km. of site
- ○ Cycle trail – direct access from site
- ☑ Cycle trail access within 2 km. of site
- ☑ Mountain bike track within 2 km. of site
- ○ Bicycle hire on site
- ○ Accompanied hiking trips
- ○ Accompanied cycling trips
- ○ Drying room for wet clothes/boots
- ○ Packed lunch service

The River Tilt Park

Golf Course Road, Blair Atholl, Pitlochry PH18 5TB (Perth and Kinross)
t: 01796 481467 e: stuart@rivertilt.co.uk
alanrogers.com/UK7295 **www.rivertiltpark.co.uk**

Accommodation: ☑ Pitch ☑ Mobile home/chalet ○ Hotel/B&B ○ Apartment

This good quality, family owned park is set on the banks of the River Tilt, a short walk from the village of Blair Atholl, where the 16th-century Blair Castle stands proud. There are 54 privately owned caravan holiday homes. Two central areas have been set aside for touring caravans, motorcaravans and tents, with 31 pitches mostly with hardstanding. Divided by mature shrubs and hedges, all have 10A electricity connections, 18 have water and a drain. One of the areas is reserved for dog owners and their pets. The Steadings Spa provides an indoor pool, solarium, steam room, spa pool and multigym, plus Waves hair salon. Also open to the public, there are charges for these facilities. The park also has an award winning restaurant. Adjacent are a riverside walk and a golf course. There may be some noise from the railway line that runs alongside the park.

You might like to know

The local area proudly boasts many places of natural beauty - many easily accessible on foot. The Falls Of Bruar, Glen Tilt and The Pass of Killiecrankie are all manageable walks, attracting visitors of all ages.

☑ Walking notes or maps available
○ Waymarked footpath – direct access from site
☑ Waymarked footpath within 1 km. of site
○ Cycle trail – direct access from site
☑ Cycle trail access within 2 km. of site
☑ Mountain bike track within 2 km. of site
○ Bicycle hire on site
○ Accompanied hiking trips
○ Accompanied cycling trips
○ Drying room for wet clothes/boots
○ Packed lunch service

Facilities: The purpose built toilet block is centrally situated (with key entry) and provides en-suite toilet and washbasin cabins and individual large preset showers, one suitable for disabled visitors. Baby facilities. Well equipped laundry. Motorcaravan service point. Bar and restaurant. Leisure spa complex with indoor pool, etc. Hair salon. Tennis. WiFi throughout (free). Max. 2 dogs per pitch. Off site: Private fishing and golf adjacent. Bicycle hire 0.5 miles. Riding 1.5 miles. Pitlochry with its famous salmon leap 6 miles. Bus or train from Blair Atholl.

Open: Two weeks after Easter - 10 November.

Directions: From the A9 just north of Pitlochry, take B8079 into Blair Atholl and follow signs for River Tilt.
GPS: 56.76538, -3.83962

Charges guide

Per unit incl. 2 persons
and electricity £ 16,00 - £ 20,00

extra person	£ 1,50
child	£ 1,00
dog	£ 2,00

Facilities: The four modern toilet blocks with showers (extra showers in two blocks) and units for visitors with disabilities. An excellent block in Nevis Park (one of the eight camping fields) has some washbasins in cubicles, showers, further facilities for disabled visitors, a second large laundry room and dishwashing sinks. Motorcaravan service point. Shop (Easter-mid Oct), barbecue area and snack bar (May-mid Sept). Play area on bark. Off site: Fishing 1 mile. Golf 4 miles. Riding 4.5 miles.

Open: 15 March - 31 October.

Directions: Turn off A82 to east at roundabout just north of Fort William following camp sign.

GPS: 56.804517, -5.073917

Charges guide

Per unit incl. 2 persons
and electricity £ 16,50 - £ 22,50

extra person £ 1,80 - £ 3,20

child (5-15 yrs) £ 1,00 - £ 1,60

dog no charge

United Kingdom – Fort William

Glen Nevis Caravan & Camping Park

Glen Nevis, Fort William PH33 6SX (Highland)
t: 01397 702191 e: holidays@glen-nevis.co.uk
alanrogers.com/UK7830 www.glen-nevis.co.uk

Accommodation: ☑ Pitch ☑ Mobile home/chalet ○ Hotel/B&B ☑ Apartment

Just outside Fort William, in a most attractive and quiet situation with views of Ben Nevis, this spacious park is used by those on active pursuits as well as sightseeing tourists. It comprises eight quite spacious fields, divided between caravans, motorcaravans and tents (steel pegs required). It is licensed for 250 touring caravans but with no specific tent limits. The large touring pitches, many with hardstanding, are marked with wooden fence dividers, 174 with 13A electricity and 100 also have water and drainage. The park becomes full in the peak months but there are vacancies each day. If reception is closed (possible in low season) you site yourself. There are regular security patrols at night in busy periods. The park's own modern restaurant and bar with good value bar meals is a short stroll from the park, open to all. A well managed park with bustling, but pleasing ambiance, watched over by Ben Nevis. Around 1,000 acres of the Glen Nevis estate are open to campers to see the wildlife and explore this lovely area.

You might like to know

The Caledonian Canal is easily accessible by cycle and is an amazing Victorian engineering feat which took 20 years to build and finally connected one coast of Scotland to the other.

- ☑ Walking notes or maps available
- ○ Waymarked footpath – direct access from site
- ☑ Waymarked footpath within 1 km. of site
- ○ Cycle trail – direct access from site
- ☑ Cycle trail access within 2 km. of site
- ☑ Mountain bike track within 2 km. of site
- ○ Bicycle hire on site
- ○ Accompanied hiking trips
- ○ Accompanied cycling trips
- ○ Drying room for wet clothes/boots
- ○ Packed lunch service

Facilities: Sanitary facilities provide free hot water and showers. Baby room. Laundry with ironing facilities. Campers' kitchen. Ice pack freezing. Licensed restaurant (early booking advised). Motorcaravan services. Gas supplies. Frisbee golf. TV and games rooms. Picnic benches. Tennis. Play area. Off site: Riding, fishing, golf within 5 miles. Trekking, cycling and forest walks. Leisure centre with swimming pool, cinema, theatre and pottery shop.

Open: Easter - 28 September.

Directions: Follow the N24 from Tipperary or Cahir to Bansha. Turn on to R663 for 11 km, passing Glen Hotel after 10 km. Follow signs for Ballinacourty House.

GPS: 52.41614, -8.21047

Charges guide

Per unit incl. 2 persons and electricity € 24,00 - € 27,00
extra person € 5,00
child € 4,00

Ireland – Tipperary

Ballinacourty House Touring Park

Glen of Aherlow, Tipperary (Co. Tipperary)
t: 062 565 59 e: info@camping.ie
alanrogers.com/IR9370 www.camping.ie

Accommodation: ☑ Pitch ◯ Mobile home/chalet ☑ Hotel/B&B ☑ Apartment

Ballinacourty House and its cobble-stoned courtyard form the centrepiece of this south facing park with views of the Galtee Mountains. Accessed by a tree-lined lane, the reception area is in part of the renovated 18th-century building, as is the adjoining restaurant. The park is level with 26 touring pitches with 6A electricity and 19 grassy pitches for tents. Some areas are shaded and there are open spaces to accommodate rallies and larger groups. Self-catering cottages and B&B are also available. This tranquil site is very appealing to families with young children. It is an excellent base from which to tour the Rock of Cashel, the Mitchelstown Caves, Swiss Cottage and the towns of Tipperary, Cahir and Cashel. The management has recently begun to keep farm animals in an enclosed part of the park and intends to enhance the estate's entire old walled garden.

You might like to know

The Glen of Aherlow is a walkers' paradise offering a variety of low level loop and mountain walks. Walking and trekking holidays are the most popular activities in the area, and what better way to enjoy the natural resources of mountains, rivers, lakes, forests and scenic landscape.

- ☑ Walking notes or maps available
- ◯ Waymarked footpath – direct access from site
- ☑ Waymarked footpath within 1 km. of site
- ◯ Cycle trail – direct access from site
- ☑ Cycle trail access within 2 km. of site
- ◯ Mountain bike track within 2 km. of site
- ◯ Bicycle hire on site
- ◯ Accompanied hiking trips
- ◯ Accompanied cycling trips
- ◯ Drying room for wet clothes/boots
- ◯ Packed lunch service

Facilities: Toilet facilities, kept very clean, quite modern in design and with heating, comprise showers, washbasins with mirrors, electric points, etc. in functional units occupying two corners of the large floor space. Facilities for disabled visitors. Also in the barn are dishwashing sinks, washing machine and a fridge/freezer for campers to use. Good drive-on motorcaravan service point. Good tennis court (free). Play area. Dogs are not accepted. WiFi (free). Off site: Fishing, golf, and riding 6 km. Bicycle hire 9 km.

Open: 1 May - 30 September.

Directions: Park is 300 m. off main N24, 9.6 km. west of Clonmel, 6.4 km. east of Cahir.

GPS: 52.37663, -7.84262

Charges guide

Per unit incl. 2 persons and electricity	€ 6,50
extra person	€ 7,00
child	€ 4,50

No charge per unit.
Less 20% for groups of 4 or more.

Ireland – Cahir

The Apple Camping & Caravan Park

Moorstown, Cahir (Co. Tipperary)
t: 052 744 1459   e: con@theapplefarm.com
alanrogers.com/IR9410   www.theapplefarm.com

Accommodation: ☑ Pitch   ○ Mobile home/chalet   ○ Hotel/B&B   ○ Apartment

This fruit farm and campsite combination offers an idyllic country holiday venue in one of the most delightful situations imaginable. For touring units only, it is located off the N24, midway between Clonmel and Cahir. The park has 32 pitches in a secluded situation behind the barns; they are mostly grass with 14 hardstandings and 25 electricity connections (13A, Europlug). Entrance is by way of a 300 m. drive flanked by the orchard fields and various non-fruit tree species, which are named and of interest to guests who are free to spend time walking the paths around the farm. When we visited, strawberries were being gathered – the best we had tasted all season – and award-winning apple juice, cordials, jams, etc. are sold in the farm shop. Reception is housed with the other site facilities in a large farmyard barn. The towns of Cahir and Clonmel are of historic interest and the countryside around boasts rivers, mountains, Celtic culture and scenic drives.

You might like to know

There are a number of superb excursions on foot, or by bicycle. These include the 15th-century Moorstown Castle (3 km) and the 12th-century Cahir Castle (7 km).

- ☑ Walking notes or maps available
- ○ Waymarked footpath – direct access from site
- ☑ Waymarked footpath within 1 km. of site
- ○ Cycle trail – direct access from site
- ☑ Cycle trail access within 2 km. of site
- ☑ Mountain bike track within 2 km. of site
- ○ Bicycle hire on site
- ○ Accompanied hiking trips
- ○ Accompanied cycling trips
- ○ Drying room for wet clothes/boots
- ○ Packed lunch service

Facilities: Two blocks house the sanitary and laundry facilities and include hot showers on payment (€ 1). Small shop and takeaway service (June-Sept). Small play area. Fishing and boat launching. Off site: Riding 1 km. Bicycle hire and golf 10 km. Small beach near and Derrynane Hotel with bar and restaurant.

Open: All year.

Directions: On the N70 (Ring of Kerry), 1.5 km. east of Caherdaniel.

GPS: 51.75881, -10.09112

Charges guide

Per unit incl. 2 persons and electricity € 27,00	
extra person € 6,00	
child € 2,00	

Ireland – *Caherdaniel*

Wave Crest Caravan & Camping Park

Caherdaniel (Co. Kerry)
t: 066 947 5188 e: wavecrest@eircom.net
alanrogers.com/IR9560 www.wavecrestcamping.com

Accommodation: ☑ Pitch ○ Mobile home/chalet ○ Hotel/B&B ○ Apartment

It would be difficult to imagine a more dramatic location than Wave Crest's on the Ring of Kerry coast. Huge boulders and rocky outcrops tumble from the park entrance on the N70 down to the seashore which forms the most southern promontory on the Ring of Kerry. There are spectacular southward views from the park across Kenmare Bay to the Beara peninsula. Sheltering on grass patches in small coves that nestle between the rocks and shrubbery, are 65 hardstanding pitches and 20 on grass offering seclusion. Electricity connections are available (13A). This park would suit older people looking for a quiet, relaxed atmosphere. A unique feature is the TV room, an old stone farm building with a thatched roof. Its comfortable interior includes a stone fireplace heated by a converted cast iron marker buoy. Caherdaniel is known for its cheerful little pubs and distinguished restaurant. The Derrynane National Park Nature Reserve is only a few kilometres away.

You might like to know

There are some fine local walks with commanding views of beaches, coves and distant mountains. You may catch a view of basking sharks and dolphins.

- ☑ Walking notes or maps available
- ○ Waymarked footpath – direct access from site
- ☑ Waymarked footpath within 1 km. of site
- ○ Cycle trail – direct access from site
- ☑ Cycle trail access within 2 km. of site
- ○ Mountain bike track within 2 km. of site
- ○ Bicycle hire on site
- ○ Accompanied hiking trips
- ○ Accompanied cycling trips
- ○ Drying room for wet clothes/boots
- ○ Packed lunch service

Facilities: Modern toilet facilities include showers on payment. En-suite unit for campers with disabilities. Laundry room. Campers' kitchen. Shop. Takeaway (8/7-25/8). TV lounge. Tennis. Play area. Picnic area. Games room. Security patrol. Off site: Fishing and golf 2 km. Riding 3 km. Bicycle hire 5 km. Woodland walk into Killarney. A visit to Killarney National Park is highly recommended.

Open: 1 April - 30 September.

Directions: Approaching Killarney from all directions, follow signs for N72 Ring of Kerry/Killorglin. At last roundabout join R562/N72. Continue for 5.5 km. and Fossa is the second park to the right.

GPS: 52.07071, -9.58573

Charges guide

Per unit incl. 2 persons and electricity	€ 22,00 - € 26,00
extra person	€ 6,00
child (under 16 yrs)	€ 2,50
hiker/cyclist incl. tent	€ 8,00 - € 9,00

Ireland – Killarney

Fossa Caravan & Camping Park

Fossa, Killarney (Co. Kerry)
t: 064 663 1497   e: fossaholidays@eircom.net
alanrogers.com/IR9590   www.fossacampingkillarney.com

Accommodation: ✔ Pitch   ✔ Mobile home/chalet   ◯ Hotel/B&B   ✔ Apartment

This park is in the village of Fossa, ten minutes by car or bus (six per day) from Killarney town centre. Fossa Caravan Park has a distinctive reception building and hostel accommodation, a stimulating play area and shop. The park is divided in two – the touring caravan area lies to the right, tucked behind the main building and to the left is an open grass area mainly for campers. Touring pitches, with 10/15A electricity and drainage, have hardstanding and are angled between shrubs and trees in a garden setting. To the rear at a higher level and discreetly placed are 30 caravan holiday homes, sheltered by the thick foliage of the wooded slopes which climb high behind the park. Not only is Fossa convenient for Killarney (5.5 km), it is also en-route for the famed Ring of Kerry, and makes an ideal base for walkers and golfers. Less than eight kilometres away are the famous walk up the Gap of Dunloe, and Carrantuohill, the highest mountain in Ireland.

You might like to know

Fossa is located on the Kerry Way. Killarney National Park, Gap of Dunloe, MacGillycuddy Reeks are all within easy distance of the site.

- ✔ Walking notes or maps available
- ◯ Waymarked footpath – direct access from site
- ✔ Waymarked footpath within 1 km. of site
- ◯ Cycle trail – direct access from site
- ✔ Cycle trail access within 2 km. of site
- ◯ Mountain bike track within 2 km. of site
- ◯ Bicycle hire on site
- ◯ Accompanied hiking trips
- ◯ Accompanied cycling trips
- ◯ Drying room for wet clothes/boots
- ◯ Packed lunch service

Facilities: Toilet and shower facilities were clean when we visited. Modern and well equipped campers' kitchen and dining area. Comfortable campers' sitting room. Laundry facilities with washing machines and dryer. Motorcaravan service point. Picnic and barbecue facilities. Fishing and boat launching from site. Off site: Bicycle hire 800 m. Riding 3 km. Golf 14 km. Pubs, restaurants and shops 15 minutes walk. Watersports, bird watching, walking and photography. Local cruises to Skelligs Rock with free transport to and from the port for walkers and cyclists.

Open: 15 March - 15 October.

Directions: Park is 300 m. off the N70 Ring of Kerry road, 800 m. southwest of Cahirciveen (or Cahersiveen) on the road towards Waterville. **GPS:** 51.941517, -10.24465

Charges guide

Per unit incl. 2 persons and electricity	€ 27,00
extra person	€ 6,00

Reductions for activity groups and rallies if pre-paid. No credit cards.

Mannix Point Camping & Caravan Park

Cahirciveen (Co. Kerry)
t: 066 947 2806 e: mortimer@campinginkerry.com
alanrogers.com/IR9610 www.campinginkerry.com

Accommodation: ☑ Pitch ◯ Mobile home/chalet ◯ Hotel/B&B ◯ Apartment

A tranquil, beautifully located seashore park, it is no exaggeration to describe Mannix Point as a nature lovers' paradise. Situated in one of the most spectacular parts of the Ring of Kerry, overlooking the bay and Valentia Island, the rustic seven-acre park commands splendid views in all directions. The park road meanders through the level site and offers 42 pitches of various sizes and shapes, many with shelter and seclusion. A charming, old fisherman's cottage has been converted to provide facilities including reception, excellent campers' kitchen and a cosy sitting room with turf fire. The knowledgeable and hospitable owner is a Bord Fáilte registered local tour guide. A keen gardener, Mortimer Moriarty laid out the site over 20 years ago and his intention to cause as little disruption to nature as possible has succeeded. The site opens directly onto marshland which teems with wildlife (a two-acre nature reserve) with direct access to the beach and seashore. This is also an ideal resting place for people walking the Kerry Way.

You might like to know

You have a choice of high level or low level, long distance or short walks here. Reception are pleased to make recommendations and have plenty of maps to borrow or purchase.

- ☑ Walking notes or maps available
- ◯ Waymarked footpath – direct access from site
- ☑ Waymarked footpath within 1 km. of site
- ◯ Cycle trail – direct access from site
- ☑ Cycle trail access within 2 km. of site
- ◯ Mountain bike track within 2 km. of site
- ◯ Bicycle hire on site
- ◯ Accompanied hiking trips
- ◯ Accompanied cycling trips
- ◯ Drying room for wet clothes/boots
- ◯ Packed lunch service

Facilities:
A single modern, heated, toilet block in the touring area provides the usual facilities including good sized showers (charged) and vanity style open washbasins. Baby room. Basic facilities for disabled visitors. Laundry facilities. Dishwashing outside. Additional toilet facilities with washbasins in cubicles are located behind the touring field reception building (open July/Aug). Motorcaravan service point. Bar and snack bar. Play area. Fun pool for small children. In main park: European and Chinese restaurants, bar and snack bar, takeaways (all year). Shop (Easter-end Aug). Tennis courts and sports field. Water ski school; water ski shows (Sundays in July/Aug). Bicycle hire. Cable TV point (included) and WiFi (charged, first hour free) on all pitches. Off site: Riding 5 km. Beach 8 km. Golf and sailing 10 km.

Open: All year.

Directions: Jabbeke is 12 km. southwest of Bruges. From A18/A10 motorways, take exit 6/6B (Jabbeke). At roundabout take first exit signed for site. In 650 m. on left-hand bend, turn left to site in 600 m. Main reception is on left but in high season continue to touring site on right in 200 m.

GPS: 51.18448, 3.10445

Charges guide

Per unit incl. up to 4 persons and electricity € 20,00 - € 36,00

dog € 2,00

Belgium – Jabbeke

Recreatiepark Klein Strand

Varsenareweg 29, B-8490 Jabbeke (West Flanders)
t: 050 811 440 e: info@kleinstrand.be
alanrogers.com/BE0555 www.kleinstrand.be

Accommodation: ◉ Pitch ◉ Mobile home/chalet ○ Hotel/B&B ○ Apartment

In a convenient location just off the A10 motorway and close to Bruges, this site is in two distinct areas divided by an access road. The touring section has 137 large pitches on flat grass separated by well trimmed hedges; all have electricity and access to water and drainage. Though surrounded by mobile homes and seasonal caravans, this is a surprisingly relaxing area and the ambience was further enhanced in 2011 when a small park was created at its centre. Some children's leisure facilities are provided here, and there is a spacious bar and a snack bar with takeaway. The main site with all the privately owned mobile homes is closer to the lake, so has most of the amenities. These include the main reception building, restaurants, bar, minimarket, and sports facilities. This is a family holiday site and offers a comprehensive programme of activities and entertainment in July and August. The lake is used for water skiing and has a supervised swimming area with waterslides (high season) and a beach volleyball area.

You might like to know

Jabbeke is located at the heart of the picturesque Brugse Ommeland, with miles of excellent walking and cycle tracks close at hand.

- ◉ Walking notes or maps available
- ○ Waymarked footpath – direct access from site
- ◉ Waymarked footpath within 1 km. of site
- ○ Cycle trail – direct access from site
- ◉ Cycle trail access within 2 km. of site
- ○ Mountain bike track within 2 km. of site
- ◉ Bicycle hire on site
- ○ Accompanied hiking trips
- ○ Accompanied cycling trips
- ○ Drying room for wet clothes/boots
- ○ Packed lunch service

Facilities: Three modern, heated toilet blocks are well equipped with some washbasins in cabins and have facilities for disabled visitors. Hairdryer. Laundry facilities. Motorcaravan services. Washing machine. Bar. Restaurant. TV room. Tennis. Play area. Multisport terrain. Pétanque. Bicycle hire. Tourist information. Mobile homes for rent (one adapted for disabled users). Free WiFi over site. Off site: Walking and cycling tracks. Golf. Antwerp. Bobbejaanlaand amusement park

Open: All year.

Directions: Approaching from Antwerp, head east on A21/E34 motorway as far as exit 24 (Turnhout). Leave here and head south on N19 to Kasterlee, and then west on N123 to Lichtaart. Follow signs to the site.

GPS: 51.21136, 4.90298

Charges guide

Per unit incl. 2 persons	€ 13,95 - € 19,90
extra person	€ 4,70
child (3-11 yrs)	€ 3,30
dog (max. 1)	€ 3,80

Belgium – Lichtaart

Camping Floréal Kempen

Herentalsesteenweg 64, B-2460 Lichtaart (Antwerp)
t: 014 556 120   e: kempen@florealgroup.be
alanrogers.com/BE0665   www.florealgroup.be/page/kempen-lichtaart.html

Accommodation: ☑ Pitch   ☑ Mobile home/chalet   ○ Hotel/B&B   ○ Apartment

This is an attractive woodland site and a member of the Floréal group. It is located close to the well known Purperen Heide, a superb nature reserve with 15 scenic footpaths leading through it. There are 228 pitches, of which only 32 are reserved for touring units. These are of a good size (100 sq.m. or more), all with 16A electricity and most with their own water supply. Two simple cabins are available for hikers, as well as fully equipped mobile homes. There are some good leisure facilities, including tennis and a multisports pitch, as well as a popular bar and restaurant. Day trips to Antwerp are very much a possibility. The old city is a gem with a great deal of interest, including over a thousand noted monuments, a diamond museum and the Rubens trail. Another popular visit is to the charming Bobbejaanlaand amusement park. There are miles of forest trails and the site's friendly managers will be pleased to recommend routes.

You might like to know

A number of hiker's cabins are available for rent on a one-night basis – ideal for those attempting some of the region's excellent long-distance footpaths.

- ☑ Walking notes or maps available
- ○ Waymarked footpath – direct access from site
- ☑ Waymarked footpath within 1 km. of site
- ○ Cycle trail – direct access from site
- ☑ Cycle trail access within 2 km. of site
- ☑ Mountain bike track within 2 km. of site
- ☑ Bicycle hire on site
- ○ Accompanied hiking trips
- ○ Accompanied cycling trips
- ○ Drying room for wet clothes/boots
- ○ Packed lunch service

Facilities: All the facilities that one would expect of a large site are available. Showers are free, washbasins both open and in cabins. Baby room. Laundry room with washing machines and dryers. Shop, restaurant, bar and takeaway (2/4-5/11). Heated outdoor swimming pool (1/5-1/9), paddling pool and slide. Sports field. Tennis. Bicycle hire. Playground and club for children. Entertainment programme during school holidays. Varied activity programme, including archery, canoeing, climbing, abseiling and walking. WiFi (charged). Off site: La Roche en Ardennes and Baraque de Fraiture (ski resort) 10 km. Golf 20 km.

Open: All year.

Directions: From E25/A26 autoroute (Liège-Luxembourg) take exit 50 then the N89 southwest towards La Roche. After 8 km. turn right (north) on N841 to Dochamps where site is signed.

GPS: 50.23127, 5.62583

Charges guide

Per unit incl. 2 persons and electricity	€ 21,20 - € 42,20
extra person (over 4 yrs)	€ 4,25 - € 7,25
dog (high season max. 1)	€ 2,00 - € 5,00

Belgium – Dochamps

Panoramacamping Petite Suisse

Al Bounire 27, B-6960 Dochamps (Luxembourg)
t: 084 444 030 e: info@petitesuisse.be
alanrogers.com/BE0735 www.petitesuisse.be

Accommodation: ⊘ Pitch ⊘ Mobile home/chalet ○ Hotel/B&B ○ Apartment

This quiet site is set in the picturesque countryside of the Belgian Ardennes, a region in which rivers flow through valleys bordered by vast forests where horses are still usefully employed. Set on a southerly slope, the site is mostly open and offers wide views of the surrounding countryside. The 193 touring pitches, all with 10A electricity, are either on open sloping ground or in terraced rows with hedges in between, and trees providing some separation. Gravel roads provide access around the site. To the right of the entrance barrier a large wooden building houses reception, a bar and a restaurant. Close by is an attractive, heated outdoor swimming pool with wide terraces surrounded by grass. Behind this is a large play area adjoining a small terrace. Although the site has many activities on offer, the opportunity should not be missed to make excursions into the countryside with its hills and forests. The villages offer small inviting bars and restaurants.

You might like to know

Petite Suisse is located at the heart of the Belgian Ardennes close to the villages of Durbuy and La Roche en Ardenne. There is usually plenty of snow in the winter and cross-country skiing is popular. The ski area of Baraque de Fraiture is 8 km away.

- ⊘ Walking notes or maps available
- ○ Waymarked footpath – direct access from site
- ⊘ Waymarked footpath within 1 km. of site
- ○ Cycle trail – direct access from site
- ⊘ Cycle trail access within 2 km. of site
- ⊘ Mountain bike track within 2 km. of site
- ⊘ Bicycle hire on site
- ○ Accompanied hiking trips
- ○ Accompanied cycling trips
- ○ Drying room for wet clothes/boots
- ○ Packed lunch service

Facilities: A newly constructed, centrally located toilet block is between the touring and long stay areas. It can be heated in cool weather and provides washbasins in cubicles and controllable hot showers on payment. Washing machine. No facilities for disabled campers. A further older unit is at the end of the mill building. Restaurant and bar with hotel (8 rooms). Mill museum. Off site: Town facilities 800 m.

Open: 1 April - 11 November.

Directions: From town centre take N89 south towards St Hubert, turning right towards Hives where site is signed. Site is 800 m. from the town centre.

GPS: 50.17362, 5.57750

Charges guide

Per unit incl. 2 persons
and electricity € 16,40 - € 18,50

extra person € 2,70

dog € 2,00

Camping le Vieux Moulin

Petite Strument 62, B-6980 La Roche-en-Ardenne (Luxembourg)
t: 084 411 380 e: info@strument.com
alanrogers.com/BE0770 www.strument.com

Accommodation: ☑ Pitch ◯ Mobile home/chalet ☑ Hotel/B&B ◯ Apartment

Located in one of the most beautiful valleys in the heart of the Ardennes, le Vieux Moulin has 183 pitches and, although there are 127 long stay units at the far end of the site, the 60 touring pitches do have their own space. Some are separated by hedges, others for tents and smaller units are more open, all are on grass, and there are 50 electricity hook-ups (6A). The 19th-century watermill has been owned and operated by the owner's family for many years, but has now been converted into a small hotel and a fascinating mill museum. Visits are possible with an audio guide in English. La Roche is a pretty little town in an unspoiled area, a very scenic region of rolling tree-clad hills and small deep valleys, with rocks for climbing, castles to explore and rivers to fish.

You might like to know

Various other sports are on offer here including canoeing, tennis and even parascending.

☑ Walking notes or maps available
◯ Waymarked footpath – direct access from site
☑ Waymarked footpath within 1 km. of site
◯ Cycle trail – direct access from site
☑ Cycle trail access within 2 km. of site
◯ Mountain bike track within 2 km. of site
◯ Bicycle hire on site
◯ Accompanied hiking trips
◯ Accompanied cycling trips
◯ Drying room for wet clothes/boots
◯ Packed lunch service

Facilities:
Heated sanitary block with showers and washbasins in cabins. Facilities for disabled visitors. Motorcaravan service point. Laundry. Bar, restaurant, takeaway (open all season). Baker calls daily. Games/TV room. Sports field with play equipment. Boules. Bicycle hire. Golf weeks. Discounts on six local 18-hole golf courses. WiFi over site. Apartments to rent. Off site: Bus to Clervaux and Vianden stops (4 times daily) outside site entrance. Riding 5 km. Castle at Vianden 14 km. Monastery at Clervaux 14 km. Golf 15 km.

Open: 30 March - 4 November.

Directions: Take N7 north from Diekirch. At Hosingen, turn right onto the narrow and winding CR324 signed Eisenbach. Follow site signs from Eisenbach or Obereisenbach.

GPS: 50.01602, 6.13600

Charges guide

Per unit incl. 2 persons
and electricity € 19,90 - € 28,00

extra person € 5,00

dog € 3,00

Luxembourg – Eisenbach

Camping Kohnenhof

Kounenhaff 1, L-9838 Eisenbach
t: 929 464 e: kohnenhof@pt.lu
alanrogers.com/LU7680 www.campingkohnenhof.lu

Accommodation: ☑ Pitch ☑ Mobile home/chalet ○ Hotel/B&B ○ Apartment

Nestling in a valley with the River Our running through it, Camping Kohnenhof offers a very agreeable location for a relaxing family holiday. From the minute you stop at the reception you are assured of a warm and friendly welcome. There are 105 pitches, 80 for touring, all with 6/16A electricity. Numerous paths cross through the wooded hillside so this could be a haven for walkers. A little bridge crosses the small river over the border to Germany. The river is shallow and safe for children (parental supervision essential). A large sports field and play area with a selection of equipment caters for younger campers. During the high season, an entertainment programme is organised for parents and children. The owner organises special golf weeks with games on different courses and discounts have been agreed at several local courses (contact the site for details). The restaurant is part of an old farmhouse and offers a wonderful ambience to enjoy a meal.

You might like to know

There are several outstanding hiking trails close at hand including the GR5, which ends in Nice, and the classic pilgrims' route (E3) to Santiago de Compostela.

- ○ Walking notes or maps available
- ○ Waymarked footpath – direct access from site
- ☑ Waymarked footpath within 1 km. of site
- ○ Cycle trail – direct access from site
- ☑ Cycle trail access within 2 km. of site
- ☑ Mountain bike track within 2 km. of site
- ☑ Bicycle hire on site
- ○ Accompanied hiking trips
- ○ Accompanied cycling trips
- ○ Drying room for wet clothes/boots
- ○ Packed lunch service

Facilities:
Bar, restaurant and snack bar (all season). Swimming and paddling pools (15/5-1/9). Playground. Activiities organised in high season. WiFi (free). Off site: Adventure park in village. 'Parc Merveilleux' funfair and Zoo, karting, bowling, National Mine Museum, preserved steam train. Fishing and bicycle hire 2 km. Golf 8 km. Riding 10 km. Arlon 10 km. Luxembourg 18 km.

Open: All year.

Directions: On A4/E25 from Belgium into Luxembourg, take first exit (no. 1) after the border. Follow signs to Steinfort (N4). Entrance to site is on the left just before the village (opposite petrol station).

GPS: 49.6583, 5.927

Charges guide

Per unit incl. 2 persons
and electricity € 15,30 - € 23,00

extra person € 4,25 - € 5,00

child (2-10 yrs) € 3,40 - € 4,00

dog € 0,85 - € 1,00

Luxembourg – Steinfort

Camping Steinfort

72 rue de Luxembourg, L-8440 Steinfort
t: 398 827 e: campstei@pt.lu
alanrogers.com/LU7720 www.camping-steinfort.lu

Accommodation: ◉ Pitch ◉ Mobile home/chalet ○ Hotel/B&B ○ Apartment

Close to the Belgian border and convenient for the motorway route from Brussels to Luxembourg City, this could be useful for an overnight stay or for a longer visit to explore Luxembourg and southern Belgium. It is a pleasant site on the edge of the village of Steinfort with a choice of open or shady pitches and is open all year, as is its restaurant. Of the 142 pitches, 80 are for touring (all with electricity 16A and water), 4 units for hire and 56 private. The site becomes lively in high season, when numerous activities are organised for children and adults. Walkers and cyclists can head straight out into the countryside and a fishing lake and an adventure park are nearby. The village centre is a short walk away and a neighbouring village has a good supermarket well known for its fresh fish counter. For a wide range of shopping, cultural and leisure activities, the bustling city of Luxembourg is along the motorway to the east. Historic Arlon is just across the border in Belgium.

You might like to know

Sandwiches can be purchased opposite the campsite.

- ◉ Walking notes or maps available
- ○ Waymarked footpath – direct access from site
- ◉ Waymarked footpath within 1 km. of site
- ◉ Cycle trail – direct access from site
- ○ Cycle trail access within 2 km. of site
- ○ Mountain bike track within 2 km. of site
- ○ Bicycle hire on site
- ○ Accompanied hiking trips
- ○ Accompanied cycling trips
- ◉ Drying room for wet clothes/boots
- ○ Packed lunch service

Facilities: Four excellent sanitary blocks provide showers (token € 0.75), washbasins (in cabins and communal) and children and baby rooms with small toilets, washbasins and showers. Laundry. Parking and service area for motorcaravans. Well stocked shop. Bar. Restaurant and takeaway. Swimming pools. Beauty salon. Playgrounds. Cross-country skiing when snow permits. Bicycle hire. Children's club. WiFi throughout (charged). Off site: Castles, museums and walks all within a reasonable distance. Bus stops outside site entrance. Riding 500 m. Bowling 1 km. Fishing 3 km. Supermarket and shops in Ettelbruck 7 km.

Open: All year.

Directions: Take N15 from Diekirch to Heiderscheid. Site is on left at top of hill just before reaching the village. Motorcaravan service area is signed on the right.

GPS: 49.87750, 5.99283

Charges guide

Per unit incl. 2 persons and electricity	€ 20,00 - € 35,00
extra person	€ 3,00
child (under 4 yrs)	€ 1,00 - € 2,00
dog	€ 3,00

Camping Fuussekaul

4 Fuussekaul, L-9156 Heiderscheid
t: 268 8881 e: info@fuussekaul.lu
alanrogers.com/LU7850 www.fuussekaul.lu

Accommodation: ☑ Pitch ☑ Mobile home/chalet ○ Hotel/B&B ☑ Apartment

This site lies in the rolling wooded hills of central Luxembourg, not far from the lakes of the Sûre river dam. Of the 370 pitches, 220 of varying sizes are for touring units, all with a 6/16A electricity connection. There are some super pitches with private electricity and water. The site consists of winding roads, some sloping, along which the pitches are set in shaded areas. The touring area (separate from the chalets and seasonal pitches) is well equipped with modern facilities, although there is no provision for visitors with disabilities. Children who visit Fuussekaul won't want to leave as there is so much for them to do. There is a fun pool, a paddling pool, exciting play areas, and an entertainment programme for all ages. This includes little shows and theatre productions, and various sporting activities. On the opposite side of the road is Camping Reenert, a naturist site owned by the same people and permitted to use the Fuussekaul facilities. There is also a supermarket with daily fresh bread, a shop for campers, fitness centre, wellness centre and hairdresser.

You might like to know

This is a heavily wooded area with some excellent trails leading through the forest to pretty rural villages.

- ☑ Walking notes or maps available
- ○ Waymarked footpath – direct access from site
- ☑ Waymarked footpath within 1 km. of site
- ○ Cycle trail – direct access from site
- ☑ Cycle trail access within 2 km. of site
- ○ Mountain bike track within 2 km. of site
- ☑ Bicycle hire on site
- ○ Accompanied hiking trips
- ○ Accompanied cycling trips
- ○ Drying room for wet clothes/boots
- ○ Packed lunch service

Facilities: Three clean, modern toilet blocks have family showers, hot water (on payment) and dishwashing sinks. One block has facilities for disabled visitors and a small laundry. Café/snack bar. Half size billiard tables. Play area. Football pitch. Tennis. Volleyball. Minigolf. Activities for children up to 12 yrs. (high season). Bicycle hire. Tourist information. WiFi over part of site (charged). Off site: Shops and restaurants in Bergen op Zoom. Golf and riding 2 km. Sailing and boat launching 4 km. Fishing 5 km. Watersports. Walking and cycle tracks.

Open: 1 May - 1 October.

Directions: Approaching from the south (Antwerp) use A4 motorway as far as the Bergen op Zoom exit and then follow signs to the Binnenschelde and campsite.

GPS: 51.469064, 4.322337

Charges guide

Per unit incl. 2 persons and electricity	€ 18,50
extra person	€ 3,00
child (3-10 yrs)	€ 2,00
dog	€ 3,00

Camping Uit en Thuis

Heimolen 56, NL-4625 DD Bergen op Zoom (Noord-Brabant)
t: 0164 233 391 e: info@campinguitenthuis.nl
alanrogers.com/NL5539 www.campinguitenthuis.nl

Accommodation: ◉ Pitch ◉ Mobile home/chalet ○ Hotel/B&B ○ Apartment

Camping Uit en Thuis (home and away) is a friendly, family run site close to the town of Bergen op Zoom. There is a choice of 80 sunny or shady touring pitches. Most pitches have electricity (6A), water, drainage and cable TV connections. A number of fully equipped mobile homes are available for rent, as well as a simply furnished hikers' cabin (maximum three nights). There are also several pitches for cycle campers. On-site amenities include a popular snack bar/restaurant, which specialises in traditional Dutch cuisine (including frikandels and various schnitzels). Bergen op Zoom is a pleasant Burgundian town, which was granted city status in 1266. It is a delightful place to explore with numerous historic buildings, many surrounding the Grote Markt, including the Markiezenhof Palace, which is now home to the city's cultural centre. The city borders the Binnenschelde Lake, popular for windsurfing and other watersports. Further afield, the surrounding Brabant countryside offers some excellent opportunities for walking and cycling.

You might like to know

This site is uniquely situated on the outskirts of Bergen op Zoom on the Brabantse Wal, a varied, undulating landscape of forest and heathland between Zeeland and North Brabant. Endless walking and cycling opportunities.

- ◉ Walking notes or maps available
- ◉ Waymarked footpath – direct access from site
- ◉ Waymarked footpath within 1 km. of site
- ◉ Cycle trail – direct access from site
- ◉ Cycle trail access within 2 km. of site
- ◉ Mountain bike track within 2 km. of site
- ◉ Bicycle hire on site
- ◉ Accompanied hiking trips
- ◉ Accompanied cycling trips
- ○ Drying room for wet clothes/boots
- ○ Packed lunch service

Facilities: Modern clean toilet block with all necessary facilities. Washing machine/dryer. Outdoor swimming pool. Café. Terrace. Play area. Boules. Large chess set. Small sandy river beach and boat ramp. Bicycle hire. Motorcaravan services. Fishing. WiFi (charged). Dogs are welcome in a small area of the site and limited to one dog per pitch. Off site: Gelderse Poort National Park. Arnhem, many ancient buildings, shops, bars, cafés, zoo. World War II museum. Nijmegen, the Netherlands' oldest city. Many marked walks and cycle tracks. Boating on river. River ferries.

Open: 1 April - 1 October.

Directions: Leave A15 motorway at Bemmel between Nijmegen and Arnhem, signed Gendt (7 km). Site is signed from Gendt.

GPS: 51.87597, 5.98897

Charges guide

Per unit incl. 2 persons
and electricity € 26,00

extra person € 5,00

dog € 3,50

No credit cards.

Camping Waalstrand

Waaldijk 23A, NL-6691 MB Gendt (Gelderland)
t: 0481 421 604   e: info@waalstrand.nl
alanrogers.com/NL5823   www.waalstrand.nl

Accommodation: ⊘ Pitch   ○ Mobile home/chalet   ○ Hotel/B&B   ○ Apartment

Camping Waalstrand lies just outside the village of Gendt. It is stretched out along the banks of the River Waal and backed by a dyke separating the river from the town. Many of the pitches have good views of the various boats plying the river. Surrounding the campsite is an excellent nature reserve, the Gelderese Poort, an extensive delta of river dunes, lowland forests and meadows with many walks and cycle routes. This is a quiet campsite with no organised entertainment. There are 150 medium size, level, unshaded, grassy pitches with 90 for touring. All pitches have 6A electricity and a TV hook-up. Access is good for large outfits. The campsite has a pleasant snack bar and a terrace overlooking the river. The swimming pool and beach area make it an excellent site for children, and within a short distance are the well known ancient cities of Arnhem and Nijmegen. Gendt, the local town, has a supermarket and various shops and restaurants.

You might like to know

The site lies in the Gelderse Poort National Park with its beautiful views over the River Waal. It is ideal for walking and cycling, and an extensive network of routes start from the site (www.lekkerfietsen.nl). In June, visitors will receive a complimentary map.

- ⊘ Walking notes or maps available
- ○ Waymarked footpath – direct access from site
- ○ Waymarked footpath within 1 km. of site
- ⊘ Cycle trail – direct access from site
- ○ Cycle trail access within 2 km. of site
- ○ Mountain bike track within 2 km. of site
- ⊘ Bicycle hire on site
- ○ Accompanied hiking trips
- ○ Accompanied cycling trips
- ○ Drying room for wet clothes/boots
- ○ Packed lunch service

Facilities
Facilities: Modern heated toilet block including facilities for babies, families and disabled visitors. Washing machines and dryers. Well stocked shop, bread to order. TV room/library. Playground with large sandpit. Bicycle hire. Boules. Hikers' cabins. WiFi over site (charged). Off site: Good restaurant within walking distance. Burgers zoo. Shops and restaurants in Arnhem. Riding 3 km. Golf 4 km. Museums and castles. Many cycle and walking tracks throughout wooded estate.

Open: 28 March - 28 October.

Directions: From Utrecht follow the A12 and take exit N224 following signs towards Arnhem Noord/Burgers zoo. Follow signs to the site.

GPS: 52.0072, 5.87135

Charges guide

Per unit incl. 2 persons
and electricity € 17,90 - € 20,40

extra person € 4,25 - € 4,70

child (under 13 yrs) € 2,40 - € 2,65

dog € 2,70 - € 3,00

Netherlands – Arnhem

Camping Warnsborn

Bakenbergseweg 257, NL-6816 PB Arnhem (Gelderland)
t: 0264 423 469 e: info@campingwarnsborn.nl
alanrogers.com/NL5830   www.campingwarnsborn.nl

Accommodation: ⊘ Pitch ⊘ Mobile home/chalet ○ Hotel/B&B ○ Apartment

Camping Warnsborn is a small, well maintained site set in the grounds of an attractive estate owned by the Gelderland Trust for natural beauty. Located on the outskirts of the historical city of Arnhem and set amongst 3.5 hectares of undulating woodland, this site really has something for everyone. There are 90 hardstanding pitches for tourers (6A electricity) arranged in either open grassy fields or surrounded by trees, with a separate secluded area for backpackers and small tents. On-site facilities include a good play area with a large sandpit and guided walks through the surrounding countryside, taking in local historical points of interest. This is an ideal site for those seeking tranquillity in a delightful, natural setting, just 4 km. from Arnhem. The city is well worth a visit, with many good parks, museums, shops and restaurants. Also popular is Burgers Zoo, one of the largest in the Netherlands, and featuring an underwater walkthrough, mangrove and rainforest.

You might like to know

Many cycling and walking routes start direct from the site. There is a tent field at the edge, where walkers and cyclists can always find a spot. Expect a warm welcome from Felix and Margo!

- ⊘ Walking notes or maps available
- ⊘ Waymarked footpath – direct access from site
- ○ Waymarked footpath within 1 km. of site
- ⊘ Cycle trail – direct access from site
- ○ Cycle trail access within 2 km. of site
- ⊘ Mountain bike track within 2 km. of site
- ⊘ Bicycle hire on site
- ⊘ Accompanied hiking trips
- ○ Accompanied cycling trips
- ○ Drying room for wet clothes/boots
- ○ Packed lunch service

Facilities: Two modern toilet blocks have open style washbasins and preset hot showers. Children's facilities and a baby room. Washing machine. Motorcaravan service point. Bar, restaurant and snack bar (1/4-30/9). Children's pool. Play equipment. Football. Volleyball. Riding. Bicycle hire. WiFi over site (charged). Off site: Outdoor swimming pool. Golf 1 km. Fishing 2 km. National parks. Hiking, mountain biking and riding. Appelscha.

Open: 1 April - 31 October.

Directions: From A28 take exit 31 and follow N381 towards Drachten/Appelscha. Take the exit for Appelscha, then follow signs to the site.

GPS: 52.94579, 6.362007

Charges guide

Per unit incl. 2 persons and electricity	€ 17,50 - € 20,50
extra person	€ 2,50
dog (max 1)	€ 2,50 - € 3,00

Camping Alkenhaer

Alkenhaer 1, NL-8426 EP Appelscha (Friesland)
t: 0516 432 600 e: info@campingalkenhaer.nl
alanrogers.com/NL6085 www.campingalkenhaer.nl

Accommodation: ☑ Pitch ☑ Mobile home/chalet ○ Hotel/B&B ○ Apartment

Alkenhaer is a pleasant and peaceful family campsite near Appelscha in the southeast part of Friesland, and close to the province of Drenthe. Located between the beautiful natural parks of Drents-Friese Wold and Fochteloërveen, the focus is very much on space and nature. The 240 pitches, 90 for touring, are dispersed over spacious marked fields and are all equipped with 10A electricity. The fields only take a few units, making camping here cosy. Shade is provided by mature trees. There are separate hardstanding areas for mobile homes and large caravans. On-site amenities include a large football field, a volleyball court, a well equipped playground and a children's pool. In high season, there are a variety of activities organised by a professional team. Off site, Appelscha is a delightful village dating back to the 13th century. The fortunes of the site are linked to the peat trade, and in the 19th century coastal erosion led to the establishment of a large forest. Thanks to this forest and the sand dunes beyond it, Appelscha has become an important holiday centre.

You might like to know

Alkenhaer is located between two national parks: Drents-Friese Wold and Fochteloërveen, both unique nature reserves. The pleasant village of Appelscha can be easily reached on foot.

☑ Walking notes or maps available
○ Waymarked footpath – direct access from site
☑ Waymarked footpath within 1 km. of site
☑ Cycle trail – direct access from site
○ Cycle trail access within 2 km. of site
☑ Mountain bike track within 2 km. of site
☑ Bicycle hire on site
☑ Accompanied hiking trips
○ Accompanied cycling trips
○ Drying room for wet clothes/boots
○ Packed lunch service

Facilities: New sanitary facilities have washbasins in cubicles and hot showers (key operated). No facilities for children or disabled visitors. Well stocked shop (fresh bread daily), takeaway, bar and restaurant (weekends only in low season). High class restaurant/brasserie (all year). Playgrounds. Lakeside beach and swimming. Well stocked fishing lake. Bicycle hire. Max. 2 dogs. Public transport is 5 min. walk away. WiFi (charged). Only gas barbecues permitted. Riding. Off site: Golf 20 km.

Open: 15 March - 27 October.

Directions: Leave A15 at exit 35 and take N233 towards Kesteren. After 2 km. turn left then right onto N320. After 1 km. turn right at signpost and then first right. Site is on left in 1 km. New entrance 200 m. past old entrance (closed).

GPS: 51.93753, 5.54589

Charges guide

Per unit incl. 2 persons and electricity	€ 21,00 - € 27,00
extra person	€ 5,00
dog	€ 5,00

Camping Betuwe

Hoge Dijkseweg 40, NL-4041 AW Kesteren (Gelderland)
t: 0488 481 477 e: info@campingbetuwe.nl
alanrogers.com/NL6275 www.campingbetuwe.nl

Accommodation: ✅ Pitch ✅ Mobile home/chalet ⭕ Hotel/B&B ✅ Apartment

Camping Betuwe is in the Neder-Betuwe municipality of Gelderland, a rich agricultural region of fruit plantations and tree nurseries. This long established park is undergoing a complete transformation. As well as the many seasonal pitches, there are spacious pitches for touring units and tents, with 16A hook-up, adjacent to the new toilet facilities. There are two lakes, one with a sandy beach and play area and the other being a well stocked fishing lake. This site is suitable for all ages, for those seeking peace and tranquillity in rural surroundings, and for families with young children and teenagers. A convivial bar and restaurant with takeaway also provides a varied entertainment programme during the high season. For that special occasion there is the newly opened brasserie. The park has a well stocked shop where fresh bread rolls are available each morning.

You might like to know

Cycle or walk through the beautiful spring blossom of the Betuwe, well known for its fruit production. There are miles of walking routes along the riverbanks.

✅ Walking notes or maps available
⭕ Waymarked footpath – direct access from site
⭕ Waymarked footpath within 1 km. of site
✅ Cycle trail – direct access from site
⭕ Cycle trail access within 2 km. of site
⭕ Mountain bike track within 2 km. of site
✅ Bicycle hire on site
⭕ Accompanied hiking trips
⭕ Accompanied cycling trips
⭕ Drying room for wet clothes/boots
✅ Packed lunch service

Recreatiepark De Boshoek

Harremaatweg 34, NL-3781 NJ Voorthuizen (Gelderland)
t: 0342 471 297 e: info@deboshoek.nl
alanrogers.com/NL6337 www.deboshoek.nl

Accommodation: ☑ Pitch ☑ Mobile home/chalet ☑ Hotel/B&B ○ Apartment

Facilities: One clean, heated toilet block has free showers and some washbasins in cubicles. Good facilities for children and disabled visitors. Some private sanitary facilities to rent on pitches. Mini market. Restaurant, bar, snack bar. Large swimming complex. Sauna and Turkish steam bath. Large adventure play area for children. Pony riding and lessons. Minigolf. 10-pin bowling. Short golf. Tennis. Football. Basketball. Children's farm. Entertainment and children's club. Hairdresser. Bicycle hire. WiFi over part of site (charged). Off site: Walking and cycling in the National Park. Old cities of Apeldoorn and Amersfoort. Kröller-Müller Museum (one of the world's largest collections of Van Gogh paintings).

Open: 23 March - 27 October.

Directions: Approaching on A1 motorway, take exit 16 and drive to Voorthuizen. In Voorthuizen at first roundabout turn right and drive through the village. Then take first turn right (Bosweg). At the end turn left to the site entrance on the right (500 m).

GPS: 52.187556, 5.630970

Charges guide

Per unit incl. 2 persons
and electricity € 22,00 - € 35,00

private sanitary facilites € 8,00 - € 10,00

extra person € 5,00

No credit cards.

Camping de Boshoek is a spacious, family oriented campsite, which forms part of a large leisure park that includes bungalows for rent and private chalets. There are 130 touring pitches of 100-120 sq.m, all equipped with 10A electricity, water, drainage and cable TV connections. They are in various fields, each with its own play area and including two car-free areas, with a central area for general use. There are eight pitches reserved for campers. Rented accommodation includes comfortable safari tents equipped with kitchen, terrace and a private bathroom. Children will enjoy the playground with its giant 7.5-metre slide. There is also a pony club and a children's farm. The sports park includes an interactive soccer wall and many other amenities for all age groups, including minigolf, crossbow archery and short golf. Voorthuizen is a small town close to the site, while Amersfoort, Apeldoorn and the Hoge Veluwe National Park are all easily visited by car.

You might like to know

You can cycle to your heart's content in the acres of state forest that are close to the site.

☑ Walking notes or maps available
○ Waymarked footpath – direct access from site
☑ Waymarked footpath within 1 km. of site
○ Cycle trail – direct access from site
☑ Cycle trail access within 2 km. of site
○ Mountain bike track within 2 km. of site
☑ Bicycle hire on site
○ Accompanied hiking trips
☑ Accompanied cycling trips
○ Drying room for wet clothes/boots
☑ Packed lunch service

Recreatiepark Het Winkel

De Slingeweg 20, NL-7115 AG Winterswijk (Gelderland)
t: 0543 513025 e: info@hetwinkel.nl
alanrogers.com/NL6412 www.hetwinkel.com

Accommodation: ⊘ Pitch ⊘ Mobile home/chalet ○ Hotel/B&B ⊘ Apartment

Camping Het Winkel is a friendly family campsite in the middle of unspoilt countryside, surrounded by woodland in the Achterhoek region. The generous pitches have water and electricity plus there are caravans, chalets and studio apartments to rent. Some meadow areas (without electricity) are only for tents. There are large open spaces for leisure and sporting activities and a wide range of facilities for all the family. Cycling, running and walking routes start from the site. The Achterhoek region has the most extensive network of cycle paths in the Netherlands. There is a wide variety of sporting opportunities and in the high season there is an activity programme for children of all ages. There are many interesting places to visit nearby such as Erve Brookert which is a picturesque, historic building from 1875, originally a farmhouse, hayloft and klompenhuis where clogs were made, and now is open to the public, with a tea garden (limited opening).

You might like to know

Het Winkel is located in an area classified as 'national landscape' with direct access to the longest network of sand roads in the Netherlands, ideal for cycling and hiking. Various types of bicycles are available to hire.

⊘ Walking notes or maps available
⊘ Waymarked footpath – direct access from site
⊘ Waymarked footpath within 1 km. of site
⊘ Cycle trail – direct access from site
⊘ Cycle trail access within 2 km. of site
⊘ Mountain bike track within 2 km. of site
⊘ Bicycle hire on site
○ Accompanied hiking trips
○ Accompanied cycling trips
○ Drying room for wet clothes/boots
⊘ Packed lunch service

Facilities: Modern sanitary facilities throughout. Private en-suite facilities to rent for some pitches. Children's sanitary block. Heated (1/5-15/9) outdoor adult and children's pools with sauna, water slide and solarium. Children's indoor play area. Shop, bar, restaurant. WiFi (charged). Bicycle hire. Tennis. Table tennis. Volleyball. Basketball. Terrace. Small animal park. Off site: Fishing 1 km. Riding 2 km. Golf 4 km. Running, cycling and walking tracks from site.

Open: All year.

Directions: Site is 60 km. east of Arnhem close to the border with Germany. From Winterswijk take A319 southeast for 2 km. then turn right onto De Slingeweg. Site is on outskirts of Winterswijk Brinkheurne.
GPS: 51.952137, 6.736899

Charges guide

Per unit incl. 2 persons and electricity	€ 18,00 - € 25,50
extra person	€ 3,25
dog	€ 3,00

Facilities: Two large sanitary buildings (one new for 2012) with showers, toilets, washbasins in cabins, facilities for babies and for disabled visitors. Laundry room. Spacious reception area with supermarket, restaurant, bar and takeaway. Heated pool with children's pool and sliding roof. Lake swimming with sandy beach. New modern adventure play area and smaller play areas. Pétanque. Bicycle hire. Fishing pond. Tennis. Pets to stroke. Max. 1 dog. Luxury bungalows to rent (good views). New water spray park for children up to 13 yrs. Free WiFi over site. Off site: Riding 11 km. Golf 16 km.

Open: 29 March - 1 October.

Directions: From the A1 take exit 32 (Oldenzaal-Denekamp) and continue to Denekamp. Pass Denekamp and turn right at village of Noord-Deuringen and follow signs to site.

GPS: 52.39200, 7.04900

Charges guide

Per unit incl. 2 persons and 4A electricity	€ 27,00
incl. full services	€ 30,50
extra person	€ 4,25

Netherlands – Denekamp

Camping De Papillon

Kanaalweg 30, NL-7591 NH Denekamp (Overijssel)
t: 0541 351 670 e: info@depapillon.nl
alanrogers.com/NL6470 www.depapillon.nl

Accommodation: ☑ Pitch ☑ Mobile home/chalet ○ Hotel/B&B ○ Apartment

De Papillon is perhaps one of the best and most enjoyable campsites in the Netherlands. All 245 touring pitches are spacious (120-160 sq.m), all have electricity (4/10/16A), and 220 have water and drainage. An impressive, new sanitary block has state-of-the-art equipment and uses green technology. There is a new entertainment centre with outdoor auditorium for children, and the water play area by the adventure playground and covered, heated pool is among the most imaginative and exciting we have seen. The restored heathland area offers opportunities for nature lovers; there is also a large fishing lake and a swimming lake with beach area and activities. This friendly, welcoming site is well thought through with an eye for detail and an appreciation of nature. Waste water from the showers is used to flush the toilets, all buildings are heated by solar energy, and all waste is separated for recycling. This is a great destination for a holiday amongst nature and the countryside of the Twente region. A member of Leading Campings group.

You might like to know

There is a wonderful network of cycle tracks through Twente. Good maps are available at reception.

- ☑ Walking notes or maps available
- ○ Waymarked footpath – direct access from site
- ○ Waymarked footpath within 1 km. of site
- ○ Cycle trail – direct access from site
- ☑ Cycle trail access within 2 km. of site
- ○ Mountain bike track within 2 km. of site
- ☑ Bicycle hire on site
- ○ Accompanied hiking trips
- ○ Accompanied cycling trips
- ○ Drying room for wet clothes/boots
- ○ Packed lunch service

Camping & Speelparadijs Beringerzand

Heide 5, NL-5981 NX Panningen (Limburg)
t: 0773 072 095 e: info@beringerzand.nl
alanrogers.com/NL6525 www.beringerzand.nl

Accommodation: ☑ Pitch ☑ Mobile home/chalet ○ Hotel/B&B ○ Apartment

Facilities: Four heated toilet blocks include bathrooms for children and a fully equipped launderette. Well stocked supermarket, bar, restaurant and takeaway (all open all season). Games and TV rooms. Indoor and outdoor swimming pools (not guarded). Tennis. Minigolf. Pétanque. Adventure play areas. Bicycle hire. Small BMX track. Outdoor chess. Riding. Fishing. Children's club and evening entertainment. WiFi throughout (charged). Max. 2 dogs per pitch. Off site: Golf 2 km.

Open: 28 March - 2 November.

Directions: From the A67 between Eindhoven and Venlo take exit 38 (direction Helden). At lights turn right to Koningslust and after 2 km. turn right again to site following camping signs.
GPS: 51.34897, 5.96101

Charges guide

Per unit incl. 2 persons
and electricity (plus meter) € 31,75

extra person € 5,00

dog € 4,85

No credit cards.

The history of this friendly site dates back more than 100 years to when it was established as a holiday resort for members of the Lazarist religious congregation. The park and its historic building (now the Patershof restaurant) have, for the last 40 years, been developed as a holiday paradise for young families. Beringerzand is set amongst the lovely villages and small lakes of the wooded area between the De Peel Natural Park and the Muse river. The 21-hectare site offers 375 spacious touring pitches, all with electricity (10A), TV, water and waste water, arranged around the edges of green fields. There are currently also 140 privately owned chalets. The fields have been very well designed and include various activity areas appropriate to different age groups. Very good amenities provide activities in both good and bad weather with indoor and outdoor pools, an indoor play centre and a variety of sports. The Patershof restaurant is very special with good value meals and room for children to play and read books.

You might like to know

The site is located in the south of the Netherlands, in the Peel and Maas area, where you can walk over wooden bridges through the marshes. One of the cycle maps will guide you along the River Maas and the Maasplassen at Roermond.

- ☑ Walking notes or maps available
- ☑ Waymarked footpath – direct access from site
- ☑ Waymarked footpath within 1 km. of site
- ☑ Cycle trail – direct access from site
- ☑ Cycle trail access within 2 km. of site
- ☑ Mountain bike track within 2 km. of site
- ☑ Bicycle hire on site
- ○ Accompanied hiking trips
- ○ Accompanied cycling trips
- ☑ Drying room for wet clothes/boots
- ☑ Packed lunch service

Facilities: Four well spaced sanitary units are well equipped and of good quality. Facilities for disabled visitors, bathrooms and baby rooms shared between the units. Hot water is charged (€ 0.50) except in the washbasins (some in cubicles). Laundry room. Shop (all season but less hours in low season as is restaurant/bar and café). Children's play equipment on sand and grass. Swimming at lake within walking distance. Charcoal barbecues are not permitted. A limited number of dogs are accepted (check with site). WiFi throughout (charged). Off site: Discounts arranged for local attractions such as the zoo, swimming pool and amusement park (if booked at reception).

Open: 28 March - 25 October.

Directions: From A28 take exit for Maarn and follow signs to site.

GPS: 52.079868, 5.381638

Charges guide

Per unit incl. 2 persons
and electricity € 17,00 - € 20,50

Netherlands – Woudenberg

Vakantiepark De Heigraaf

De Heygraeff 9, NL-3931 ML Woudenberg (Utrecht)
t: 0332 865 066   e: info@heigraaf.nl
alanrogers.com/NL6910   www.heigraaf.nl

Accommodation: ⊘ Pitch ⊘ Mobile home/chalet ○ Hotel/B&B ○ Apartment

This family run site in a central Netherlands rural environment is very close to a public lake with sandy beaches set in pine woods, catering well for families. With this popular attraction within walking distance, the site has a fairly high proportion of residential mobile homes and seasonal caravans but provides 200 marked pitches for touring units out of the overall 500. Accessed by a central tarmac road these are nicely situated around the edges of small hedged field areas on level grass, with electricity (4/16A) available to most. The newer area at the top of the site has individual pitches (some with toilet units) with young hedging overlooking the fields. The main facility area in the centre of the site provides entertainment for children during school holidays with a pleasant café area and the usual small animal enclosure popular with the Dutch. The reception at the site entrance is in the traditional farmhouse and offers good local information. Some English is spoken. There are many walks and cycle ways and the site is also well situated for visiting Amsterdam (60 km).

You might like to know

De Heigraaf is in the Utrechtse Heuvelrug on the edge of the Gelderse Vallei, a perfect location for good walking and cycling. Winding through the forests, you can enjoy the fresh air, nature at its best and – in some places – an overwhelming silence.

- ⊘ Walking notes or maps available
- ⊘ Waymarked footpath – direct access from site
- ⊘ Waymarked footpath within 1 km. of site
- ⊘ Cycle trail – direct access from site
- ⊘ Cycle trail access within 2 km. of site
- ⊘ Mountain bike track within 2 km. of site
- ⊘ Bicycle hire on site
- ○ Accompanied hiking trips
- ○ Accompanied cycling trips
- ⊘ Drying room for wet clothes/boots
- ○ Packed lunch service

Facilities: One large and two smaller heated toilet blocks in traditional style provide separate toilets, showers and washing cabins. High standards of cleanliness, a dedicated unit for disabled campers and provision for babies. Warm water is free of charge. Dishwasher. Launderette. Motorcaravan services. Supermarket, snack bar, restaurant and takeaway (all season). Recreation room. Youth centre. Tennis. Playground and play field. Animal farm. Bicycle and children's pedal hire. Canoe, surf, pedal boat and boat hire. Fishing. WiFi over site (charged). Two cottages for hikers. No dogs allowed. Off site: Golf 3 km. Riding 6 km. Beach 7 km.

Open: 28 March - 30 September.

Directions: From the Amsterdam direction take the A4 (Europoort), then the A15 (Europoort). Take exit for Brielle on N57 and, just before Brielle, site is signed.

GPS: 51.9097, 4.18536

Charges guide

Per unit incl. 2 persons and electricity	€ 18,00 - € 25,00
extra person	€ 3,30
child (under 12 yrs)	€ 2,80

Netherlands – Brielle

Camping De Krabbeplaat

Oude Veerdam 4, NL-3231 NC Brielle (Zuid-Holland)
t: 0181 412 363 e: info@krabbeplaat.nl
alanrogers.com/NL6980 www.krabbeplaat.nl

Accommodation: ☑ Pitch ☑ Mobile home/chalet ○ Hotel/B&B ○ Apartment

Camping De Krabbeplaat is a family run site situated near the ferry port in a wooded, recreation area next to the Brielse Meer lake. There are 448 spacious pitches, with 68 for touring units, all with electricity (10A), cable connections and a water supply nearby. A nature conservation plan exists to ensure the site fits into its natural environment. The lake and its beaches provide the perfect spot for watersports and relaxation and the site has its own harbour where you can moor your own boat. This excellent site is very convenient for the Europort ferry terminal. Plenty of cultural opportunities can be found in the historic towns of the area. Because of the large range of amenities and the tranquil nature of the site, De Krabbeplaat is perfect for families and couples.

You might like to know

At Oostvoorne, at the tip of the island, lies the unique Voornes Dune. Due to the direct influence of the sea, there are plants growing in this nature reserve that are not found elsewhere in Europe.

- ☑ Walking notes or maps available
- ○ Waymarked footpath – direct access from site
- ○ Waymarked footpath within 1 km. of site
- ○ Cycle trail – direct access from site
- ☑ Cycle trail access within 2 km. of site
- ○ Mountain bike track within 2 km. of site
- ☑ Bicycle hire on site
- ○ Accompanied hiking trips
- ○ Accompanied cycling trips
- ○ Drying room for wet clothes/boots
- ○ Packed lunch service

Facilities: Three modern toilet blocks with washbasins in cabins and controllable hot showers. Family shower rooms. Children's section. Baby room. En-suite facilities for disabled visitors. Laundry. Campers' kitchen. Motorcaravan services. Shop (all season). Playground. Minigolf. Fishing. Archery. Watersports and boat launching. Pétanque. TV room. Play house with Lego and Play Station. Daily activities for children in high season. WiFi (charged). Torch useful. English is spoken. Off site: Riding 3 km. Golf 8 km. Bicycle hire 15 km.

Open: Week before Easter - 30 October.

Directions: From German/Danish border follow E45 north. Take exit 69 and follow to Hoptrup. From Hoptrup follow to Diernæs and Diernæs Strand.

GPS: 55.15029, 9.4969

Charges guide

Per person	DKK 71
child (under 12 yrs)	DKK 47
pitch	DKK 41 - 72
electricity	DKK 35
dog	DKK 10

Vikær Strand Camping

Dundelum 29, Diernæs, DK-6100 Haderslev (Sønderjylland)
t: 74 57 54 64 e: info@vikaercamp.dk
alanrogers.com/DK2022 www.vikaercamp.dk

Accommodation: ☑ Pitch ☑ Mobile home/chalet ○ Hotel/B&B ○ Apartment

Vikær Strand Camping in Southern Jutland lies in beautiful surroundings, right on the Diernæs Bugt beaches – ideal for both active campers and relaxation seekers. There are 390 grass pitches (210 for touring units), all with 10/16A electricity and separated by low hedges. Access is from long, gravel lanes. Forty newly developed, fully serviced pitches have electricity, water, drainage, TV aerial point and Internet. From these, and from the front pitches on the lower fields, there are marvellous views over the Diernæs Bugt. A Blue Flag beach runs along one edge of the site, and it can be narrow in places. It is well used for beach games, paddling and swimming. For the active there are several routes for walking and cycling and, of course, sea fishing trips are possible. In the area are a newly developed swamp nature reserve, Schackenborg Castle and the battlefields of Dybbøl Banke.

You might like to know

Why not join in the Midsummer celebrations here – with live entertainment until midnight and a spectacular bonfire.

☑ Walking notes or maps available
○ Waymarked footpath – direct access from site
☑ Waymarked footpath within 1 km. of site
○ Cycle trail – direct access from site
☑ Cycle trail access within 2 km. of site
○ Mountain bike track within 2 km. of site
○ Bicycle hire on site
○ Accompanied hiking trips
○ Accompanied cycling trips
○ Drying room for wet clothes/boots
○ Packed lunch service

Facilities:
Two partly refurbished toilet blocks have British style toilets, washbasins in cabins and controllable hot showers. Children's section and baby room. Family shower rooms. Facilities for disabled visitors. Fully equipped laundry. Campers' kitchen. Motorcaravan service point. Shop. Café/grill with bar and takeaway (evenings). Swimming pool (80 sq.m) with paddling pool. Sauna and solarium. Play area and adventure playground. Games room with satellite TV. Minigolf. Fishing. Watersports. Off site: Golf and riding 5 km.

Open: 15 March - 20 September.

Directions: From Århus follow the 15 road towards Grenå and then the 16 road towards town centre. Turn north and follow signs for Fornæs and the site.

GPS: 56.45602, 10.94107

Charges guide

Per person DKK 85	
child (1-12 yrs) DKK 45	
electricity (10A) DKK 35	
dog DKK 15	

Credit cards 5% surcharge.

Denmark – Grenå

Fornæs Camping

Stensmarkvej 36, DK-8500 Grenå (Århus)
t: 86 33 23 30 e: fornaes@1031.inord.dk
alanrogers.com/DK2070 www.fornaesfamiliecamping.dk

Accommodation: ✔ Pitch ✔ Mobile home/chalet ○ Hotel/B&B ○ Apartment

In the grounds of a former farm, Fornæs Camping is about 5 km. from Grenå. From reception, a wide gravel access road descends through a large grassy field to the sea. Pitches to the left are mostly level, to the right slightly sloping with some terracing and views of the Kattegat. The rows of pitches are divided into separate areas by colourful bushes and each row is marked by a concrete tub containing a young tree and colourful flowers. Fornæs has 320 pitches of which 240 are for tourers, the others being used for seasonal visitors. All touring pitches have 10A electricity. At the foot of the site is a pebble beach with a large grass area behind it for play and sunbathing. There is also an outdoor pool with two slides, a paddling pool, sauna, solarium and whirlpool. A comprehensive room serves as a restaurant, takeaway and bar, and in a former barn there is a new games room. Fornæs provides a good base from which to explore this part of Denmark.

You might like to know

Den Gamle By ('The Old Town'), founded in 1909, was the world's first open-air museum of urban history and culture. Seventy-five historic houses from all over Denmark shape the contours of a Danish town as it might have looked in the days of Hans Christian Anderson.

- ✔ Walking notes or maps available
- ○ Waymarked footpath – direct access from site
- ✔ Waymarked footpath within 1 km. of site
- ○ Cycle trail – direct access from site
- ✔ Cycle trail access within 2 km. of site
- ○ Mountain bike track within 2 km. of site
- ○ Bicycle hire on site
- ○ Accompanied hiking trips
- ○ Accompanied cycling trips
- ○ Drying room for wet clothes/boots
- ○ Packed lunch service

Facilities:
Facilities: Two good, large, heated toilet blocks are central, with spacious showers and some washbasins in cubicles. Separate children's room. Baby rooms. Bathrooms for families (some charged) and disabled visitors. Laundry. Well equipped kitchens and barbecue areas. TV lounges. Motorcaravan services. Pizzeria. Supermarket, restaurant and bar (all season). Pool complex. Wellness centre with sauna, solariums, whirlpool bath, fitness room and indoor play hall. TV rental. Play areas. Crèche. Bicycle hire. Cabins to rent. WiFi over part of site (charged). Off site: Golf 10 km. Boat launching 25 km.

Open: 30 March - 21 October.

Directions: Turn off Thisted-Fjerritslev 11 road to Klim from where site is signed.

GPS: 57.133333, 9.166667

Charges guide

Per unit incl. 2 persons
and electricity € 31,00 - € 50,30

extra person € 11,00

child (1-11 yrs) € 8,20

Denmark – Fjerritslev

Klim Strand Camping

Havvejen 167, Klim Strand, DK-9690 Fjerritslev (Nordjylland)
t: 98 22 53 40   e: ksc@klim-strand.dk
alanrogers.com/DK2170   www.klim-strand.dk

Accommodation: ☑ Pitch   ☑ Mobile home/chalet   ○ Hotel/B&B   ○ Apartment

A large family holiday site right beside the sea, Klim Strand is a paradise for children. It is a privately owned TopCamp site with a full complement of quality facilities, including its own fire engine and trained staff. The site has 460 numbered touring pitches, all with electricity (10A), laid out in rows, many divided by trees and hedges, with shade in parts. Some 220 of these are extra large (180 sq.m) and fully serviced with electricity, water, drainage and TV hook-up. On-site activities include an outdoor water slide complex, an indoor pool, tennis, pony riding and a kayak school. A wellness spa centre including an indoor play hall is a recent addition. There are numerous play areas, an adventure playground with aerial cable ride and a roller skating area. Live music and dancing are organised twice a week in high season. Suggested excursions include trips to offshore islands, visits to local potteries, a brewery museum and birdwatching on the Bygholm Vejle.

You might like to know

After a day's walking or cycling you can enjoy being pampered at the site's first rate wellness and spa centre.

☑ Walking notes or maps available
○ Waymarked footpath – direct access from site
☑ Waymarked footpath within 1 km. of site
○ Cycle trail – direct access from site
☑ Cycle trail access within 2 km. of site
○ Mountain bike track within 2 km. of site
☑ Bicycle hire on site
○ Accompanied hiking trips
○ Accompanied cycling trips
○ Drying room for wet clothes/boots
○ Packed lunch service

Lærdal Ferie & Fritidspark

Grandavegens, N-6886 Lærdal (Sogn og Fjordane)
t: 57 66 66 95 e: info@laerdalferiepark.com
alanrogers.com/NO2375 www.laerdalferiepark.com

Accommodation: ☑ Pitch ☑ Mobile home/chalet ☑ Hotel/B&B ☑ Apartment

This site is beside the famous Sognefjord, the longest fjord in the world. It is ideally situated if you want to explore the glaciers, fjords and waterfalls of the region. The 100 pitches are level with well trimmed grass, connected by tarmac roads and are suitable for tents, caravans and motorcaravans. There are 80 electrical hook-ups. The fully licensed restaurant serves traditional, locally sourced meals as well as snacks and pizzas. The pretty little village of Lærdal, only 400 m. away, is well worth a visit. A walk among the old, small wooden houses is a pleasant and interesting experience. You can hire boats on the site for short trips on the fjord. Guided hiking, cycling and fishing trips are also available, with waymarked cycling and walking trails running through the park. Climbing excursions can be arranged on request. The site also provides 29 traditional Norwegian cabins, flats and rooms to rent, plus a motel, all very modern and extremely tastefully designed.

You might like to know

There are some great hikes in the area – enjoy a fantastic accompanied walk from the fjord to the mountain summit with stunning views of Lærdal.

- ☑ Walking notes or maps available
- ◯ Waymarked footpath – direct access from site
- ☑ Waymarked footpath within 1 km. of site
- ◯ Cycle trail – direct access from site
- ☑ Cycle trail access within 2 km. of site
- ☑ Mountain bike track within 2 km. of site
- ☑ Bicycle hire on site
- ☑ Accompanied hiking trips
- ☑ Accompanied cycling trips
- ◯ Drying room for wet clothes/boots
- ◯ Packed lunch service

Facilities: Two modern and well decorated sanitary blocks with washbasins (some in cubicles), showers on payment, and toilets. Facilities for disabled visitors. Children's room. Laundry facilities. Kitchen. Motorcaravan services. Small shop, bar, restaurant and takeaway (all 1/5-30/9). TV room. Playground. Fishing. Motorboats, rowing boats, canoes, bicycles and pedal cars for hire. Bicycle hire. Go-kart sales. Free WiFi over site. Off site: Cruises on the Sognefjord 400 m. The Norwegian Wild Salmon Centre 400 m. Riding 500 m. Golf 12 km. Skiing 20 km. The Flåm railway 40 km.

Open: All year,
by telephone request 1 Nov - 14 March.

Directions: Site is on road 5 (from the Oslo-Bergen road, E16) 400 m. north of Lærdal village centre.
GPS: 61.10037, 7.46986

Charges guide

Per unit incl. 2 persons and electricity	NOK 240
extra person	NOK 50
child (4-18 yrs)	NOK 25 - 37

Facilities: A modern, high quality sanitary building has washbasins in cubicles, and a feature children's room. Baby room. Facilities for disabled visitors. Kitchen with cooking facilities, dishwasher, a dining area overlooking the fjord, and laundry facilities. Motorcaravan service point. Small shop (20/6-20/8). Satellite TV, WiFi over site (free). Cabins and apartments for hire. Off site: Hiking, glacier walks, climbing, rafting, walking around Sognefjord. Details from reception. Bicycle hire 3 km.

Open: All year.

Directions: Site is off the Rv 5, 3 km. east of Sogndal, 8 km. west of Kaupanger. Access is via a short, narrow lane with passing places.

GPS: 61.21157, 7.12110

Charges guide

Per unit incl. 2 persons and electricity	NOK 270
extra person	NOK 15
child (4-16 yrs)	NOK 10

Norway – Sogndal

Kjørnes Camping

N-6856 Sogndal (Sogn og Fjordane)
t: 57 67 45 80 e: camping@kjornes.no
alanrogers.com/NO2390 www.kjornes.no

Accommodation: ◉ Pitch ◉ Mobile home/chalet ○ Hotel/B&B ◉ Apartment

Kjørnes Camping is idyllically situated on the Sognefjord, three kilometres from the centre of Sogndal. It occupies a long open meadow which is terraced down to the waterside. The site has 100 pitches for camping units (all with electricity), 14 cabins and two apartments for rent. Located at the very centre of the 'fjord kingdom' by the main no. 5 road, this site is the ideal base from which to explore the Sognefjord. You are within easy reach of all the major attractions including the Jostedal glacier, the Nærøyfjord, the Flåm Railway, the Urnes Stave Church and Sognefjellet. This site is ideal for those who enjoy peace and quiet, renowned local walks, lovely scenery or a spot of fishing with a bonus of evening sunshine. Local activities include organised guided walks on glaciers, access to several stave churches and a goat farm in the mountains. A pleasant drive takes you to Solvorn and a car park in the village from where a ferry crosses the fjord to Urnes Stave Church.

You might like to know

Why not try a glacier walk combined with kayaking on the glacier lake. Accompanied trips are available with or without overnight accommodation.

- ◉ Walking notes or maps available
- ○ Waymarked footpath – direct access from site
- ◉ Waymarked footpath within 1 km. of site
- ○ Cycle trail – direct access from site
- ◉ Cycle trail access within 2 km. of site
- ◉ Mountain bike track within 2 km. of site
- ○ Bicycle hire on site
- ◉ Accompanied hiking trips
- ○ Accompanied cycling trips
- ○ Drying room for wet clothes/boots
- ○ Packed lunch service

Trollveggen Camping

Horgheimseidet, N-6300 Åndalsnes (Møre og Romsdal)
t: 71 22 37 00 e: post@trollveggen.no
alanrogers.com/NO2452 www.trollveggen.no

Accommodation: ☑ Pitch ☑ Mobile home/chalet ○ Hotel/B&B ☑ Apartment

Facilities: One heated toilet block provides washbasins, some in cubicles, and showers on payment. Family room with baby bath and changing mat, plus facilities for disabled visitors. Communal kitchen with cooking rings, small ovens, fridge and sinks (free hot water). Laundry facilities. Motorcaravan service point. Car wash facility. Barbecue area (covered). Playground. Duck pond. Fishing. Free WiFi over site. Old Trollveggen Station Master's apartment for hire by arrangement. Off site: Waymarked walks from site. Climbing, glacier walking and hiking. Fjord fishing. Sightseeing trips. The Troll Road. Mardalsfossen (waterfall). Geiranger and Åndalsnes.

Open: 10 May - 20 September.

Directions: Site is located on the E136 road, 10 km. south of Åndalsnes. It is signed.

GPS: 62.49444, 7.758333

Charges guide

Per unit incl. 2 persons and electricity NOK 235

extra person (over 4 yrs) NOK 15

The location of this site provides a unique experience – it is set at the foot of the famous vertical cliff of Trollveggen (the Troll Wall), which is Europe's highest vertical mountain face. The site is pleasantly laid out in terraces with level grass pitches. The facility block, four cabins and reception are all very attractively built with grass roofs. Beside the river is an attractive barbecue area where barbecue parties are sometimes arranged. This site is a must for people who love nature. The site is surrounded by the Troll Peaks and the Romsdalshorn Mountains with the rapid river of Rauma flowing by. Close to Reinheimen (home of reindeer) National Park, and in the beautiful valley of Romsdalen you have the ideal starting point for trips to many outstanding attractions such as Trollstigen (The Troll Road) to Geiranger or to the Mardalsfossen waterfalls. In the mountains there are nature trails of various lengths and difficulties. The campsite owners are happy to help you with information.

You might like to know

The Romsdal Alps area offers numerous hiking trails, many close to the site. Romsdalseggen, in particular, is a very popular hike, with wonderful views of the mountains and the Romsdal valley. From Trollveggen Camping you can cycle along local roads to Åndalsnes, 10 km. away.

- ☑ Walking notes or maps available
- ☑ Waymarked footpath – direct access from site
- ○ Waymarked footpath within 1 km. of site
- ☑ Cycle trail – direct access from site
- ○ Cycle trail access within 2 km. of site
- ○ Mountain bike track within 2 km. of site
- ☑ Bicycle hire on site
- ☑ Accompanied hiking trips
- ○ Accompanied cycling trips
- ☑ Drying room for wet clothes/boots
- ○ Packed lunch service

Facilities: Three modern, heated sanitary blocks have showers (on payment), en-suite family rooms, washing up facilities and kitchen. Facilities for disabled campers in one block. Motorcaravan services. Restaurant and takeaway (15/6-15/8). Shop (1/5-1/10). Playground. Lake swimming, boating and fishing. Trampoline. Bouncy cushion. Outdoor fitness. Beach volleyball. Barbecue area and hot tub (winter). Boat, canoe and pedalo hire. Elk safaris arranged. Climbing, rafting and canoeing courses arranged (linked with Trollaktiv). Cross-country skiing (winter). Car wash. Free WiFi. Off site: Rock climbing wall. Marked forest trails. Mineral centres and mines.

Open: All year.

Directions: Site is on route 9, 2.5 km. north of the town of Byglandsfjord on the eastern shores of the lake.

GPS: 58.68839, 7.80175

Charges guide

Per unit incl. 2 persons
and electricity NOK 245 - 275

extra person NOK 10

child (5-12 yrs) NOK 5

dog no charge

Norway – Byglandsfjord

Neset Camping

N-4741 Byglandsfjord (Aust-Agder)
t: 37 93 42 55 e: post@neset.no
alanrogers.com/NO2610 www.neset.no

Accommodation: ☑ Pitch ☑ Mobile home/chalet ○ Hotel/B&B ○ Apartment

On a semi-promontory on the shores of the 40 km. long Byglandsfjord, Neset is a well run, friendly site ideal for spending a few active days, or as a short stop en route north from the ferry port of Kristiansand (from England or Denmark). Neset is situated on well kept grassy meadows by the lake shore, with water on three sides and the road on the fourth. There are 260 unmarked pitches with electricity and cable TV, and 40 hardstandings for motorcaravans. The main building houses reception, a small shop and a restaurant with fine views over the water. The campsite has a range of activities to keep you busy, and the excellent hardstandings for motorcaravans look out onto the lake. Byglandsfjord offers good fishing (mainly trout) and the area has marked trails for cycling, riding or walking in an area famous for its minerals. Samples of these can be found in reception, and day trips to specialist exhibitions at the Mineralparken (8 km) are possible. Walking and cycling routes abound and cycles and mountain bikes can be hired from Neset.

You might like to know

There are some great walks leading from the campsite, overlooking the picturesque Lake Byglangsfjorden.

☑ Walking notes or maps available
○ Waymarked footpath – direct access from site
☑ Waymarked footpath within 1 km. of site
○ Cycle trail – direct access from site
☑ Cycle trail access within 2 km. of site
○ Mountain bike track within 2 km. of site
○ Bicycle hire on site
○ Accompanied hiking trips
○ Accompanied cycling trips
○ Drying room for wet clothes/boots
○ Packed lunch service

Röstånga Camping & Bad

Blinkarpsvägen 3, S-268 68 Röstånga (Skåne Län)

t: 043 591 064 e: nystrand@msn.com

alanrogers.com/SW2630 www.rostangacamping.se

Accommodation: ☑ Pitch ☑ Mobile home/chalet ○ Hotel/B&B ○ Apartment

Beside the Söderåsen National Park, this scenic campsite has its own fishing lake and many activities for the whole family. There are 180 large, level, grassy pitches with electricity (10A) and a quiet area for tents with a view over the fishing lake. The tent area has its own service building and several barbecue places. A large holiday home and 21 pleasant cabins are available to rent all year round. A pool complex adjacent to the site provides a 50 m. swimming pool, three children's pools and a water slide, all heated during peak season. Activities are arranged on the site in high season, including a children's club with exciting activities such as treasure hunts and gold panning, and for adults, aquarobics, Nordic walking and tennis. The Söderåsen National Park offers hiking and bicycle trails. The friendly staff will be happy to help you to plan interesting excursions in the area.

You might like to know

Why not try some Nordic walking? Equipment can be borrowed from reception.

☑ Walking notes or maps available

○ Waymarked footpath – direct access from site

☑ Waymarked footpath within 1 km. of site

○ Cycle trail – direct access from site

☑ Cycle trail access within 2 km. of site

○ Mountain bike track within 2 km. of site

○ Bicycle hire on site

○ Accompanied hiking trips

○ Accompanied cycling trips

○ Drying room for wet clothes/boots

○ Packed lunch service

Facilities: Four good, heated sanitary blocks with free hot water and facilities for babies and disabled visitors. Motorcaravan service point. Laundry with washing machines and dryers. Kitchen with cooking rings, oven and microwave. Small shop at reception. Bar, restaurant and takeaway. Minigolf. Tennis. Fitness trail. Fishing. Canoe hire. Children's club. WiFi (free). Off site: Swimming pool complex adjacent to site (free for campers as is a visit to the zoo). Golf 11 km. Motor racing track at Ring Knutstorp 8 km.

Open: 10 April - 30 September.

Directions: From Malmö: drive towards Lund and follow road no. 108 to Röstånga. From Stockholm: turn off at Östra Ljungby and take road no. 13 to Röstånga. In Röstånga drive through the village on road no. 108 and follow the signs.

GPS: 55.996583, 13.28005

Charges guide

Per unit incl. 2 persons
and electricity € 25,00 - € 33,00

Facilities: Three heated sanitary blocks provide a good supply of roomy shower cubicles, washbasins, some washbasin/WC suites and WCs. Facilities for babies and disabled visitors. Well equipped laundry room. Good kitchen with cookers, microwaves and dishwasher (free), and sinks. Hot water is free. Gas supplies. Motorcaravan services. Shop (1/5-30/8). Pizzeria, licensed restaurant and café (all 1/5-30/8). Bar (1/7-31/7). Outdoor heated swimming pool (15/5-22/8). Playgrounds. Bouncy castle. Boules. Canoe hire. Bicycle hire. Minigolf. Family entertainment and activities. Football. Off site: Golf 500 m. Riding 2 km. Fishing 4 km.

Open: 12 April - 30 September.

Directions: Cross Öland road bridge from Kalmar on road no. 137. Take exit for Öland Djurpark/Saxnäs, then follow campsite signs. Site is just north of the end of the bridge.

GPS: 56.68727, 16.48182

Charges guide

Per unit incl. electricity SEK 175 - 430

Weekend and weekly rates available.

Krono Camping Saxnäs

S-386 95 Färjestaden (Kalmar Län)
t: 048 535 700   e: info@kcsaxnas.se
alanrogers.com/SW2680   www.kcsaxnas.se

Accommodation: ☑ Pitch   ☑ Mobile home/chalet   ○ Hotel/B&B   ○ Apartment

Well placed for touring Sweden's Riviera and the fascinating and beautiful island of Öland, this family run site, part of the Krono group, has 420 marked and numbered touring pitches. Arranged in rows on open, well kept grassland dotted with a few trees, all have electricity (10/16A), 320 have TV connections and 112 also have water. An unmarked area without electricity can accommodate around 60 tents. The site has about 130 long stay units and cabins for rent. The sandy beach slopes very gently and is safe for children. Reception is efficient and friendly with good English spoken. In 2009 an outdoor heated pool and a children's pool were built at the entrance to the site. In high season children's games are organised and dances are held twice weekly, with other activities on other evenings. Nearby attractions include the 7 km. long Öland road bridge and the 400 old windmills on the island (in the 19th century there were 2,000). The southern tip of Öland, Ottenby, is a paradise for bird watchers.

You might like to know

Öland is known as the island of the sun and wind and is an enchanting area, known far beyond the borders of Sweden. There are some great walks on the island and the mainland is accessible via a bridge.

- ☑ Walking notes or maps available
- ○ Waymarked footpath – direct access from site
- ○ Waymarked footpath within 1 km. of site
- ○ Cycle trail – direct access from site
- ☑ Cycle trail access within 2 km. of site
- ○ Mountain bike track within 2 km. of site
- ☑ Bicycle hire on site
- ○ Accompanied hiking trips
- ○ Accompanied cycling trips
- ○ Drying room for wet clothes/boots
- ○ Packed lunch service

Facilities: In the older style, sanitary facilities are functional rather than luxurious, providing stainless steel washing troughs, controllable hot showers with communal changing areas, and a unit for disabled visitors. Although a little short on numbers, facilities will probably suffice at most times as the site is rarely full. Kitchen and dining room with TV, four full cookers and sinks. Laundry facilities. TV room. Minigolf. Canoe, boat and bicycle hire. Fishing.

Open: All year.

Directions: Site is off road 45 behind the tourist information office in Sveg. Site is signed.

GPS: 62.03367, 14.37250

Charges guide

Per pitch SEK 150	
electricity SEK 25	

Svegs Camping

Kyrkogränd 1, S-842 32 Sveg (Jämtlands Län)
t: 068 013 025   e: info@svegscamping.se
alanrogers.com/SW2845 www.camping.se/z32

Accommodation: ☑ Pitch ☑ Mobile home/chalet ○ Hotel/B&B ○ Apartment

On the 'Inlandsvägen' route through Sweden, the town centre is only a short walk from this neat, friendly site. Two supermarkets, a café and tourist information office are adjacent. The 80 pitches are in rows, on level grass, divided into bays by tall hedges, and with electricity (10/16A) available to 70. The site has boats, canoes and bicycles for hire, and the river frontage has a barbecue area with covered seating and fishing platforms. Alongside the river with its fountain, and running through the site is a pleasant well lit riverside walk. Places to visit include the town with its lovely church and adjacent gardens, some interesting old churches in the surrounding villages, and 16th Century Remsgården, 14 km. to the west.

You might like to know

This is big country with miles of tracks to explore – the site owners will be pleased to recommend ideas.

- ☑ Walking notes or maps available
- ○ Waymarked footpath – direct access from site
- ☑ Waymarked footpath within 1 km. of site
- ○ Cycle trail – direct access from site
- ☑ Cycle trail access within 2 km. of site
- ○ Mountain bike track within 2 km. of site
- ○ Bicycle hire on site
- ○ Accompanied hiking trips
- ○ Accompanied cycling trips
- ○ Drying room for wet clothes/boots
- ○ Packed lunch service

Facilities: Café. Restaurant. Direct lake access. Saunas. Fishing. Minigolf. Boat and canoe hire. Bicycle hire. Guided tours. Play area. Tourist information. Chalets for rent. Off site: Walking and cycle routes. Boat trips. Helvetinjärvi National Park.

Open: All year.

Directions: From Helsinki, head north on the E12 motorway to Tampere and then northeast on N63-9 to Orivesi. Then, continue north on route 66 to Ruovesi and follow signs to the site.

GPS: 61.99413, 24.069843

Charges guide

Per unit incl. 2 persons and electricity € 30,00	
extra person € 4,50	
child (under 15 yrs) € 2,00	

Finland – Ruovesi

Camping Haapasaaren Lomakylä

Haapasaarentie 5, FIN-34600 Ruovesi (Häme)
t: 044 080 0290 e: lomakyla@haapasaari.fi
alanrogers.com/FI2840 www.haapasaari.fi

Accommodation: ☑ Pitch ☑ Mobile home/chalet ☑ Hotel/B&B ○ Apartment

Haapasaaren is located on Lake Näsijärvi, around 70 km. north of Tampere in south western Finland. This is a well equipped site with a café and restaurant, a traditional Finnish outside dancing area and, of course, plenty of saunas! Rowing boats, canoes, cycles and, during the winter months, sleds are all available for rent. Fishing is very popular here. Pitches are grassy and of a good size. There is also a good range of accommodation to rent, including holiday cottages with saunas. The cosy restaurant, Jätkäinkämppä, has an attractive terrace and fine views across the lake. Alternatively, the site's café, Portinpieli, offers a range of snacks as well as Internet access. Haapasaaren's friendly owners organise a series of guided tours throughout the year. These include hiking and nature treks, berry and mushroom picking, and, during the winter, ice fishing and cross-country skiing. Helvetinjärvi National Park is one of the most dramatic areas of western Finland, and is made up of deep gorges and dense forests. Occasionally brown bears and lynx can be seen here.

You might like to know

After a vigorous day's hiking, try one of the site's traditional Finnish saunas, followed by a bracing swim in the adjacent lake.

☑ Walking notes or maps available
○ Waymarked footpath – direct access from site
☑ Waymarked footpath within 1 km. of site
○ Cycle trail – direct access from site
☑ Cycle trail access within 2 km. of site
○ Mountain bike track within 2 km. of site
☑ Bicycle hire on site
☑ Accompanied hiking trips
☑ Accompanied cycling trips
○ Drying room for wet clothes/boots
○ Packed lunch service

Finland – Oulu

Nallikari Camping

Leiritie 10, FIN-90510 Oulu (Oulu)
t: 044 703 1353 e: nallikari.camping@ouka.fi
alanrogers.com/FI2970 www.nallikari.fi

Accommodation: ☑ Pitch ☑ Mobile home/chalet ○ Hotel/B&B ○ Apartment

Facilities: The modern shower/WC blocks also provide male and female saunas, kitchen and launderette facilities. Facilities for disabled visitors. Motorcaravan service point. Playground. Reception with café/restaurant (June-Aug), souvenir and grocery shop. TV room. Free WiFi over site. Bicycle hire. Communal barbecues only. Off site: The adjacent Eden Centre provides excellent modern spa facilities where you can enjoy a day under the glass-roofed pool with its jacuzzis, saunas, Turkish baths and an Irish bath. Riding 2 km. Fishing 5 km. Golf 15 km.

Open: All year.

Directions: Leave road 4/E75 at junction with road 20 and head west down Kiertotie. Site well signed, Nallikari Eden, but continue on, just after traffic lights, cross a bridge and take the second on the right. Just before the Eden Centre turn right towards Leiritie and reception.

GPS: 65.02973, 25.41793

Charges guide

Per unit incl. 2 persons	€ 13,00 - € 26,00
extra person	€ 4,00
child (under 15 yrs)	€ 2,00
electricity	€ 4,50 - € 6,50

This is probably one of the best sites in Scandinavia, set in a recreational wooded area alongside a sandy beach on the banks of the Baltic Sea, with the added bonus of the adjacent Eden Spa complex. Nallikari provides 200 pitches, 176 with 16A electricity (seven also have water supply and drainage), plus an additional 78 cottages to rent, 28 of which are suitable for winter occupation. Oulu is a modern town, about 100 miles south of the Arctic Circle, that enjoys long, sunny and dry summer days. The Baltic, however, is frozen for many weeks in the winter and then the sun barely rises for two months. In early June the days are very long with the sun setting at about 23.30 and rising at 01.30! Nallikari, to the west of Oulu, is 3 km. along purpose built cycle paths and the town has much to offer. Nordic walking, with or without roller blades, seems to be a recreational pastime for Finns of all ages! Oulu hosts events such as the Meri Oulu Festival in July and the Oulu Music Video Festival, and forms the backdrop to the mind boggling, air guitar world championships.

You might like to know

Bicycle hire is available on site including trailers for young children.

☑ Walking notes or maps available
○ Waymarked footpath – direct access from site
☑ Waymarked footpath within 1 km. of site
○ Cycle trail – direct access from site
☑ Cycle trail access within 2 km. of site
○ Mountain bike track within 2 km. of site
☑ Bicycle hire on site
○ Accompanied hiking trips
○ Accompanied cycling trips
○ Drying room for wet clothes/boots
○ Packed lunch service

Camping Goldene Meile

Simrockweg 9-13, D-53424 Remagen (Rhineland Palatinate)
t: 026 422 2222 e: info@camping-goldene-meile.de
alanrogers.com/DE32150 www.camping-goldene-meile.de

Accommodation: ☑ Pitch ○ Mobile home/chalet ○ Hotel/B&B ○ Apartment

This site is on the banks of the Rhine between Bonn and Koblenz. Although there is an emphasis on permanent caravans, there are about 200 pitches for tourers (out of 500), most with 6A electricity and 100 with water and drainage. They are either in the central, more mature area or in a newer area where the numbered pitches of 80-100 sq.m. are arranged around an attractively landscaped, small lake. Just five are by the busy river and there may be some noise from the trains that run on the other side. Access to the river bank is through a locked gate (key from reception). Adjacent to the site is a large complex of open-air public swimming pools (small concession for campers). They claim always to find space for odd nights, except perhaps at Bank Holidays. This site is in a popular area and is busy at weekends and in high season.

You might like to know

The Rheinland Pfalz cycle trail extends for 330 km and can be accessed directly from the site.

☑ Walking notes or maps available
☑ Waymarked footpath – direct access from site
☑ Waymarked footpath within 1 km. of site
☑ Cycle trail – direct access from site
☑ Cycle trail access within 2 km. of site
☑ Mountain bike track within 2 km. of site
☑ Bicycle hire on site
○ Accompanied hiking trips
○ Accompanied cycling trips
○ Drying room for wet clothes/boots
☑ Packed lunch service

Facilities: The main toilet block is heated and well maintained, with some washbasins in cabins, showers (token) and facilities for wheelchair users. A smaller block (renovated in 2012) serves the newer pitches (no showers). Laundry and cooking facilities. Motorcaravan services. Gas. Shop, bar, restaurant and takeaway (all 1/4-30/10 and some weekends). Play areas. Entertainment for children (July/Aug). Bicycle hire. WiFi over site (charged). Main gate is closed 22.00-07.00 (also 13.00-15.00). Off site: Swimming pool complex adjacent (May-Sept). Riding 1 km. Cycling and walking in the Ahr valley. Remagen, Bonn and Cologne to visit. Boat trips on the Rhine and Mosel.

Open: All year.

Directions: Remagen is 20 km. south-southeast of Bonn. Site is beside the Rhine and is signed on the N9 road just south of Remagen.

GPS: 50.57428, 7.25189

Charges guide

Per unit incl. 2 persons and electricity	€ 24,80
extra person	€ 6,00
child (2-14 yrs)	€ 5,00
dog	€ 1,70

No credit cards.

Facilities: New sanitary block of very high quality with the usual facilities and provision for disabled visitors. Baby room. Kitchen and laundry. Family sauna room (extra charge). Play area. Bicycle hire. WiFi. Site is not suitable for American RVs. Off site: Swimming pool complex (May-Sept) and all-year restaurant and bar, both adjacent. Fishing, riding and tennis within walking distance. Golf 13 km.

Open: 16 March - 15 November.

Directions: Site is 15 km. northwest of Bitburg. From A60 (E29) take exit 6 and head south to Bitburg, then take road 50 west to Sinspelt. Finally turn north for 6 km. to Neuerburg, pass through town and follow camping signs to site 1.5 km. north of the town.
GPS: 50.02852, 6.27266

Charges guide

Per unit incl. 2 persons € 15,50	
extra person € 3,00	
child (3-15 yrs) € 2,50	
electricity (per kWh) € 0,50	
dog € 2,00	

Germany – Neuerburg

Camping In der Enz

In der Enz 25, D-54673 Neuerburg (Rhineland Palatinate)
t: 065 642 660 e: info@camping-inderenz.com
alanrogers.com/DE32370 www.camping-inderenz.com

Accommodation: ✔ Pitch   ✔ Mobile home/chalet   ○ Hotel/B&B   ○ Apartment

This site is just outside the town, next to the municipal swimming pool complex, and the enthusiastic Dutch owners give a very warm welcome that makes this a very pleasant place to stay. The site is bisected by the unfenced River Enz, which is little more than a stream at this point. The section nearest the road is occupied by 50 long stay units. The other half, on the other side of the river with its own access road, is solely for tourers. This has 66 very large, open grass pitches, all with electricity (16A), of which 32 are multi-service with water and drainage. Reception keeps basic supplies, but there is a supermarket only 1.5 km. towards the town via a traffic free path/cycleway which runs along the route of the old railway line for 5 km, passing the site. At the end of June each year, on a Sunday, 38 km. of road between Arzfeld, through Neuerburg and Sinspelt to Irrel is closed to motorised traffic. Known as the Süd Eifel Tour, only pedestrians, cyclists, wheelchair users, roller-bladers etc. are allowed to enjoy this traffic-free situation (avoid arrival or departure on this day).

You might like to know

Outside of high season, transfers to and from the site are available for a small fee.

- ✔ Walking notes or maps available
- ✔ Waymarked footpath – direct access from site
- ✔ Waymarked footpath within 1 km. of site
- ✔ Cycle trail – direct access from site
- ○ Cycle trail access within 2 km. of site
- ✔ Mountain bike track within 2 km. of site
- ○ Bicycle hire on site
- ○ Accompanied hiking trips
- ○ Accompanied cycling trips
- ○ Drying room for wet clothes/boots
- ○ Packed lunch service

Facilities: The sanitary buildings, which can be heated, are of a high standard with one section in the reception/shop building for the overnight pitches, and the remainder close to the longer stay places. Laundry. Bar. Restaurant with takeaway. TV area. Skittle alley. Shop (all amenities 1/3-31/10 and Xmas). Tennis. Fishing. Play area. Rallies welcome. Torches useful. WiFi in restaurant and reception areas. Off site: Boat trips on the Rhine and Mosel. Walking in the Hunsrück region. Cycle paths.

Open: All year.

Directions: Site is 28 km. south of Koblenz. From A61 Koblenz-Ludwigshafen road, take exit 43 Pfalzfeld and on to Hausbay where site is signed. If using sat nav enter Hausbayer Strasse in Pfalzfeld.

GPS: 50.10597, 7.56822

Charges guide

Per unit incl. 2 persons
and electricity € 17,00 - € 23,00

extra person € 7,00

child (under 17 yrs) € 3,00 - € 5,00

dog no charge - € 2,00

Germany – Pfalzfeld

Country Camping Schinderhannes

D-56291 Hausbay-Pfalzfeld (Rhineland Palatinate)
t: 067 468 0280   e: info@countrycamping.de
alanrogers.com/DE32420   www.countrycamping.de

Accommodation: ☑ Pitch   ○ Mobile home/chalet   ○ Hotel/B&B   ○ Apartment

About 30 km. south of Koblenz, between Rhine and Mosel, this site is set in a 'bowl' of land which catches the sun all day. With trees and parkland all around, it is a peaceful and picturesque setting. There are 150 permanent caravans in a separate area from 90 short stay touring pitches on hardstanding. For longer stays, an area around the lake has a further 160 numbered pitches. These are of over 100 sq.m. on grass, some with hardstanding and all with 8A electricity. You can position yourself for shade or sun. The lake is used for swimming, inflatable boats and fishing. Some breeds of dog not admitted. Country Camping could be a useful transit stop en route to the Black Forest, Bavaria, Austria and Switzerland, as well as a family holiday. High in the Hunsrück (a large area with forests, ideal for walking and cycling), Schinderhannes himself was a legendary Robin Hood-type character, whose activities were curtailed in Mainz, at the end of a rope.

You might like to know

The Schinderhannes Bike Path runs close to the campsite and is a 38 km. trail between Emmelshausen and Simmern, with some delightful countryside and picture postcard villages along the way.

- ☑ Walking notes or maps available
- ○ Waymarked footpath – direct access from site
- ☑ Waymarked footpath within 1 km. of site
- ○ Cycle trail – direct access from site
- ☑ Cycle trail access within 2 km. of site
- ○ Mountain bike track within 2 km. of site
- ○ Bicycle hire on site
- ○ Accompanied hiking trips
- ○ Accompanied cycling trips
- ○ Drying room for wet clothes/boots
- ○ Packed lunch service

Prümtal Camping Oberweis

In der Klaus 17, D-54636 Oberweis (Rhineland Palatinate)
t: 065 279 2920 e: info@pruemtal.de
alanrogers.com/DE32470 www.pruemtal.de

Accommodation: ☑ Pitch ☑ Mobile home/chalet ○ Hotel/B&B ○ Apartment

A popular and comfortable site in a pleasant valley alongside the River Prüm, this site has a very good restaurant, a modern toilet block and a swimming pool. There are 100 long-stay units grouped in a separate area at the western end of the site, with the touring area stretching out alongside the river. The 130 touring pitches are on grass, some are individual and hedged others on a more open area, all with 16A electric hook-ups. Pitches vary in size (from 30-100 sq.m) and price, and there is shade from mature trees in most parts. The restaurant is of very high quality with menus printed in German, Dutch and English, and a good range of meals to suit all tastes and budgets (all year). There is a separate bar, a pizzeria (Papa Razzo), plus a takeaway service (July/August). The heated outdoor swimming pool is free to campers.

You might like to know

Oberweis, in picturesque Eifel in the Prüm valley, is the perfect location for a holiday. Walkers and cyclists will love its peaceful forests - and the site has a host of fun activities on offer.

☑ Walking notes or maps available
☑ Waymarked footpath – direct access from site
☑ Waymarked footpath within 1 km. of site
☑ Cycle trail – direct access from site
☑ Cycle trail access within 2 km. of site
○ Mountain bike track within 2 km. of site
○ Bicycle hire on site
☑ Accompanied hiking trips
○ Accompanied cycling trips
☑ Drying room for wet clothes/boots
☑ Packed lunch service

Facilities: The main toilet block is of a high standard, heated and tiled. Well equipped, it has large controllable showers, baby facilities and a good suite for disabled campers. In 2014, a new unit with a family area and dog showers will replace the current modern, Portacabin style second unit. A third unit below the pool terrace with yet more toilets and showers opens for July/Aug. Good motorcaravan service point. Small shop with limited stock (1/4-31/10). Restaurant, bar and pizzeria. Swimming pool (1/5-7/9). Adventure style playground. Large sports field. Children's entertainment in July/Aug. River fishing. WiFi over site (charged).
Off site: Golf 6 km. Bicycle hire and riding 10 km.

Open: All year.

Directions: Oberweis is 35 km. northwest of Trier. From the A60 (E29) take exit 6, and head south to Bitburg, then B50 west for 8 km. to Oberweiss. Immediately after sharp right hand bend at entry to town turn left before river bridge and garage. Continue to end of road and site entrance is to right of pool complex.

GPS: 49.95883, 6.42385

Charges guide

Per unit incl. 2 persons and electricity	€ 22,85 - € 25,45
extra person	€ 6,30
child (4-13 yrs)	€ 3,70 - € 9,20
dog	€ 2,10

Discounts for longer stays.

© Dominik Ketz

© Hans-Jurgen Sittig

Campingpark Freibad Echternacherbrück

Mindenerstrasse 18, D-54668 Echternacherbrück (Rhineland Palatinate)
t: 065 253 40 e: info@echternacherbrueck.de
alanrogers.com/DE32480 www.echternacherbrueck.de

Accommodation: ⦿ Pitch ◯ Mobile home/chalet ◯ Hotel/B&B ◯ Apartment

This is a well organised site which sprawls for a kilometre along a bank of the Sauer river. It is a very good and popular site in the town, next to the well run municipal open-air heated pool complex. The terrain is flat, with 140 seasonal pitches and 340 numbered tourist pitches, all with access to electricity points (some Euro standard, some German, 10/16A). In high season a full programme of activities includes bingo, tournaments (darts, table tennis, etc), exercises in the swimming pool, ceramic painting and outings. Trier (25 km) and the city of Luxembourg (37 km) are within reach for a day trip.

Facilities: Three heated sanitary blocks are clean and well maintained, with showers and some washbasins in cabins. Baby rooms. Facilities for disabled visitors. Free use of laundry room. Motorcaravan service point. Bar with snacks and takeaway. Bread van every morning. Swimming pool complex and paddling pool (Whitsun-15/9). Playgrounds. Boules. Bicycle hire. River fishing. Canoeing. Organised activities (15/6-15/9). Children's club (1/5-30/9). Off site: Shop 100 m. Minigolf 200 m. Restaurants within 500 m. Indoor pool 800 m. Riding 10 km. Golf 30 km.

Open: 1 April - 15 October.

Directions: On opposite side of river is Echternach, in Luxembourg. Site signed. From east, look for small arrow on right, with Camping in red. This directs an immediate sharp left turn into a one-way street. After 200 m. turn right (by Quelle shop) to site in 100 m. just past swimming pool entrance.

GPS: 49.81207, 6.43149

Charges guide

Per unit incl. 2 persons and electricity	€ 19,20 - € 27,15
extra person	€ 4,95 - € 7,40
child (5-15 yrs)	€ 3,20 - € 4,40
dog	€ 3,30 - € 4,70

You might like to know

Walking and cycling tours start from the site on both sides of the river, and cycle paths lead to Trier (Germany's oldest city) and Luxembourg city. For longer trips, a bus will return you and your bike to site.

- ⦿ Walking notes or maps available
- ◯ Waymarked footpath – direct access from site
- ⦿ Waymarked footpath within 1 km. of site
- ⦿ Cycle trail – direct access from site
- ⦿ Cycle trail access within 2 km. of site
- ⦿ Mountain bike track within 2 km. of site
- ⦿ Bicycle hire on site
- ⦿ Accompanied hiking trips
- ◯ Accompanied cycling trips
- ◯ Drying room for wet clothes/boots
- ◯ Packed lunch service

Terrassen-Camping Alte Sägemühle

Badstrasse 57, D-79295 Sulzburg (Baden-Württemberg)
t: 076 345 51181 e: info@camping-alte-saegemuehle.de
alanrogers.com/DE34520 www.camping-alte-saegemuehle.de

Accommodation: ⊘ Pitch ◯ Mobile home/chalet ◯ Hotel/B&B ◯ Apartment

This site lies just beyond the beautiful old town of Sulzburg with its narrow streets, and is on a peaceful road leading only to a natural swimming pool (formerly the mill pond) and a small hotel. It is set in a tree-covered valley with a stream running through the centre and is divided into terraced areas, each enclosed by high hedges and trees. Electrical connections (16A) are available on 42 of the 45 large touring pitches (long leads may be necessary). The site has been kept as natural as possible and is perfect for those seeking peace and quiet. The main building by the entrance houses reception, a small shop (which stocks a good selection of local wines) and the sanitary facilities. Run by the Geuss family (Frau Geuss speaks reasonable English) the site has won awards from the state for having been kept as close to nature as possible, for example, no tarmac roads, no minigolf, no playgrounds, etc. There are opportunities for walking straight from the site into the forest, and many walks and cycle rides are shown on maps available at reception.

You might like to know

The Markgräflerland is widely considered to be one of the best hiking and cycling options in the Black Forest.

- ⊘ Walking notes or maps available
- ◯ Waymarked footpath – direct access from site
- ⊘ Waymarked footpath within 1 km. of site
- ◯ Cycle trail – direct access from site
- ⊘ Cycle trail access within 2 km. of site
- ◯ Mountain bike track within 2 km. of site
- ◯ Bicycle hire on site
- ◯ Accompanied hiking trips
- ◯ Accompanied cycling trips
- ◯ Drying room for wet clothes/boots
- ◯ Packed lunch service

Facilities: In the main building, facilities are of good quality with two private cabins, separate toilets, dishwashing, washing machine and dryer. Small shop for basics, beer and local wines (all year). Torch may be useful. New room for tent guests and motorcaravan service point. Free bus and train travel in the Black Forest for guests. Off site: Natural, unheated swimming pool adjacent (June-Aug) with discount to campers. Public transport, bicycle hire, restaurants and other shops in Sulzburg 1.5 km. Riding 3 km. Fishing 8 km. Golf 12 km. Europa Park is less than an hour away.

Open: All year.

Directions: Site is easily reached from autobahn A5/E35. Take exit 64 for Bad Krozingen, south of Freiburg, onto B3 south to Heitersheim, then through Sulzburg, or if coming from south, exit 65 through Müllheim, Heitersheim and Sulzburg. Reception is to left of road. Note: arch in Sulzburg has only 3.1 m. height clearance.

GPS: 47.83548, 7.72337

Charges guide

Per unit incl. 2 persons and electricity (plus meter)	€ 19,50 - € 22,50
extra person	€ 7,00
child (1-15 yrs)	€ 4,00

Facilities: Three good quality, heated sanitary blocks include some washbasins in cabins. Baby room. Facilities for disabled visitors. Laundry facilities. Motorcaravan services. Shop. Excellent restaurant. Takeaway (weekends and daily in high season). Wellness centre. Indoor/outdoor pool. Community room with TV. Activity programme (high season). Play areas. Boules. Tennis. Fishing. Minigolf. Barbecue. Beach bar. Petting zoo and aviary. Electric go-karts. Bicycle hire. Free WiFi in central area. Off site: Riding 1.5 km. Golf 5 km. Neuenburg, Breisach, Freiburg, Basel and the Black Forest.

Open: All year.

Directions: From autobahn A5 take Neuenburg exit, turn left, then almost immediately left at traffic lights, left at next junction and follow signs for 2 km. to site (called 'Neuenburg' on most signs).

GPS: 47.79693, 7.55

Charges guide

Per unit incl. 2 persons
and electricity € 26,00

extra person € 6,50

child (2-15 yrs) € 3,50

dog € 3,00

Discount every 10th night.

Gugel's Dreiländer Camping

Oberer Wald 3, D-79395 Neuenburg am Rhein (Baden-Württemberg)
t: 076 317 719 e: info@camping-gugel.de
alanrogers.com/DE34550 www.camping-gugel.de

Accommodation: ☑ Pitch ☑ Mobile home/chalet ○ Hotel/B&B ○ Apartment

Set in natural heath and woodland, Gugel's is an attractive site with 220 touring pitches, either in small clearings in the trees, in open areas or on a hardstanding section used for overnight stays. All have electricity (10/16A), and 40 also have water, waste water and satellite TV connections. Opposite is a meadow where late arrivals and early departures may spend the night. There may be some road noise near the entrance. The site may become very busy in high season and on bank holidays but you should always find room. The excellent pool and wellness complex add to the attraction of this all year site. There is a social room where guests are welcomed with a glass of wine and a slide presentation of the attractions of the area. The Rhine is within walking distance and there is an extensive programme of activities on offer for all ages. The site is ideally placed for enjoying and exploring the south of the Black Forest, and also for night stops when travelling from Frankfurt to Basel on the A5 autobahn.

You might like to know

The site is the starting point of a well signposted Nordic Walking course. You can borrow sticks and take part in an introduction to Nordic Walking.

☑ Walking notes or maps available

☑ Waymarked footpath – direct access from site

○ Waymarked footpath within 1 km. of site

○ Cycle trail – direct access from site

☑ Cycle trail access within 2 km. of site

○ Mountain bike track within 2 km. of site

☑ Bicycle hire on site

○ Accompanied hiking trips

○ Accompanied cycling trips

○ Drying room for wet clothes/boots

○ Packed lunch service

Alpen-Caravanpark Tennsee

Am Tennsee 1, D-82494 Krün-Obb (Bavaria (S))
t: 088 251 70 e: info@camping-tennsee.de
alanrogers.com/DE36800 www.camping-tennsee.de

Accommodation: ⊘ Pitch ○ Mobile home/chalet ○ Hotel/B&B ⊘ Apartment

Tennsee is an excellent, friendly site in truly beautiful surroundings high up (1,000 m) in the Karwendel Alps with super mountain views, and close to many famous places of which Innsbruck (44 km) and Oberammergau (26 km) are two. Mountain walks are plentiful, with several lifts close by. It is an attractive site with good facilities including 164 serviced pitches with individual connections for electricity (up to 16A and two connections), gas, TV, radio, telephone, water and waste water. The other 80 pitches all have electricity and some of these are available for overnight guests at a reduced rate. Reception and comfortable restaurants, a bar, cellar youth room and a well stocked shop are all housed in attractive buildings. Many activities and excursions are organised to local attractions by the Zick family, who run the site in a very friendly, helpful and efficient manner.

You might like to know

This is great walking country. A family member leads accompanied hikes to view the Soiernseen or the Spring flowers at Buckelwiesen.

- ⊘ Walking notes or maps available
- ○ Waymarked footpath – direct access from site
- ⊘ Waymarked footpath within 1 km. of site
- ○ Cycle trail – direct access from site
- ⊘ Cycle trail access within 2 km. of site
- ○ Mountain bike track within 2 km. of site
- ⊘ Bicycle hire on site
- ⊘ Accompanied hiking trips
- ○ Accompanied cycling trips
- ○ Drying room for wet clothes/boots
- ○ Packed lunch service

Facilities: The first class toilet block has underfloor heating, washbasins in cabins and private units with WC, shower, basin and bidet for rent. Unit for disabled guests with the latest facilities. Baby bath, dog bathroom and a heated room for ski equipment (with lockers). Washing machines, free dryers and irons. Gas supplies. Motorcaravan services. Cooking facilities. Shop. Restaurants (waiter, self-service and takeaway). Bar. Youth room. Solarium. Bicycle hire. Playground. WiFi (charged). Organised activities and excursions. Bus service to ski slopes in winter. Off site: Fishing 400 m. Riding and golf 3 km. Discounted entry at Alpspitz-Wellenbad in Garmisch-Partenkirchen and Karwendel Bad in Mittenwald.

Open: All year
excl. 6 November - 15 December.

Directions: Site is just off main Garmisch-Partenkirchen-Innsbruck road no. 2 between Klais and Krün, 15 km. from Garmisch watch for small sign Tennsee & Barmsee and turn right there for site.

GPS: 47.49066, 11.25396

Charges guide

Per unit incl. 2 persons	€ 23,00 - € 26,00
extra person	€ 7,50 - € 8,00
child (6-16 yrs)	€ 3,00 - € 4,00
electricity (per kWh)	€ 0,75
dog	€ 3,30

Senior citizens special rates (not winter).

Facilities:
Facilities: Three toilet blocks with some washbasins in cabins and free controllable hot showers. Baby room with shower. Facilities for disabled visitors in one block. Washing machine and dryer. Motorcaravan services. Bar, kiosk and takeaway. New reception has fresh bread each morning and useful tourist information. Playground. TV room. Lake with beach and swimming. Fishing. Watersports. Bicycle hire. Boat launching. Sailing and windsurfing schools. Canoe hire. WiFi. Off site: Riding 1.5 km. Golf 20 km. Schwerin, Wismar and the coast.

Open: April - September.

Directions: Site is 14 km. north-northeast of Schwerin. From 8 km. east of Schwerin, take A14 (formerly 241) north along east side of lake. Exit at Schwerin Nord and turn left towards Rampe/Cambs/Güstow. After 100 m. turn left at lights towards Retendorf and Flessnow. Follow road signs rather than sat nav.

GPS: 53.75175, 11.49628

Charges guide

Per unit incl. 2 persons and electricity	€ 22,00 - € 27,00
extra person	€ 4,00
child (4-13 yrs)	€ 2,00 - € 3,00
dog	no charge

Seecamping Flessenow

Am Schweriner See 1A, D-19067 Flessenow (Mecklenburg-West Pomerania)
t: 038 668 1491 e: info@seecamping.de
alanrogers.com/DE38120 www.seecamping.de

Accommodation: ☑ Pitch ☑ Mobile home/chalet ○ Hotel/B&B ○ Apartment

Dutch owned and in a peaceful, natural setting directly on the banks of Germany's third largest lake, Seecamping Flessenow is ideal for those seeking a relaxing holiday and also for more active campers who enjoy watersports and the many hiking and cycling routes nearby. There are 250 level, grassy pitches (170 for touring units), arranged on two rectangular fields to one side of a hardcore access lane and on a newer field to the rear of the site. Some pitches have shade from mature trees, all are numbered and separated by low wooden fences. All have 10A electricity, forty-five also have water and drainage. Centrally located on the site is a kiosk with a covered terrace that also provides a takeaway service. The numerous watersports opportunities include a windsurfing school, sailing and some boats for hire.

You might like to know

There are cycle routes around the lakes in Schwerin (42, 38 and 65 km) and a lovely trip to Wismar on the Baltic Sea (24 km).

- ☑ Walking notes or maps available
- ☑ Waymarked footpath – direct access from site
- ○ Waymarked footpath within 1 km. of site
- ☑ Cycle trail – direct access from site
- ○ Cycle trail access within 2 km. of site
- ○ Mountain bike track within 2 km. of site
- ☑ Bicycle hire on site
- ○ Accompanied hiking trips
- ☑ Accompanied cycling trips
- ○ Drying room for wet clothes/boots
- ☑ Packed lunch service

Camping & Freizeitpark LuxOase

Arnsdorfer Strasse 1, Kleinröhrsdorf, D-01900 Dresden (Saxony)
t: 035 952 56666 e: info@luxoase.de
alanrogers.com/DE38330 www.luxoase.de

Accommodation: ◉ Pitch ○ Mobile home/chalet ○ Hotel/B&B ◉ Apartment

This is a well organised and quiet site located just north of Dresden with easy access from the autobahn. The site has very good facilities and is arranged on grassland beside a lake. There is access from the site to the lake through a gate. Although the site is fairly open, trees do provide shade in some areas. There are 198 large touring pitches (plus 40 seasonal in a separate area), marked by bushes or posts on generally flat or slightly sloping grass. All have 10/16A electricity and 132 have water and drainage. At the entrance is an area of hardstanding (with electricity) for late arrivals. A brand new building provides excellent sanitary facilities, a separate washing area for children with showers in a castle and washbasins in a steam river boat which blows soap bubbles in the evening. A wellness centre includes a pool, saunas, massages, fitness room and indoor playground for children. You may swim, fish and use inflatables in the lake. A wide entertainment programme is organised for children in high season. A member of Leading Campings group.

You might like to know

The site is well located to discover such attractions by bicycle as the Baroque castle in Rammenau, the fortress at Stolpen, the gingerbread city of Pulsnitz and the beer city of Radeberg.

- ◉ Walking notes or maps available
- ○ Waymarked footpath – direct access from site
- ◉ Waymarked footpath within 1 km. of site
- ○ Cycle trail – direct access from site
- ◉ Cycle trail access within 2 km. of site
- ○ Mountain bike track within 2 km. of site
- ◉ Bicycle hire on site
- ○ Accompanied hiking trips
- ○ Accompanied cycling trips
- ○ Drying room for wet clothes/boots
- ○ Packed lunch service

Facilities: Two excellent buildings provide modern, heated facilities with private cabins, a family room, baby room, units for disabled visitors and eight bathrooms for hire. Special facilities for children with novelty showers and washbasins. Jacuzzi. Kitchen. Gas supplies. Motorcaravan services. Shop and bar (1/3-31/12) plus restaurant (15/3-31/12). Bicycle hire. Lake swimming. Sports field. Fishing. Play area. Sauna. Train, bus and theatre tickets from reception. Internet point. WiFi throughout (charged). Minigolf. Fitness room. Regular guided bus trips to Dresden, Prague etc. Off site: Riding next door (lessons available). Public transport to Dresden 1 km. Golf 7.5 km. Nearby dinosaur park, zoo and indoor karting.

Open: All year excl. February.

Directions: Site is 17 km. northeast of Dresden. From the A4 (Dresden-Görlitz) take exit 85 (Pulnitz) and travel south towards Radeberg. Pass through Leppersdorf and site is signed to the left. Follow signs for Kleinröhrsdorf and camping. Site is 4 km. from the autobahn exit.

GPS: 51.120401, 13.980103

Charges guide

Per unit incl. 2 persons and electricity	€ 19,90 - € 26,60
extra person	€ 5,00 - € 8,00
child (3-15 yrs acc. to age)	€ 2,50 - € 4,50
dog	€ 2,50 - € 3,50

Various special offers in low season.

Facilities: Modern toilet block with underfloor heating. Sauna. Mobile home for rent (max 6 people). Accommodation in luxuriously converted farm buildings. Bicycle hire. WiFi throughout (free). Off site: Bus stop 200 m. Railway station 2 km. Hiking and cycle trails. Riding 2 km. Fishing 3 km. Skiing 6 km. Golf 10 km.

Open: All year.

Directions: Vernerovice is located in the northeast of the country, just 1 km from the Polish border. From route 302 between Broumov and Mieroszow (Poland) take the exit at Mezimisti and, in Vernerovice, follow signs to the campsite.

GPS: 50.616409, 16.228651

Charges guide

Per unit incl. 2 persons and electricity € 16,50

Czech Republic – Vernerovice

Camping Aktief

Vernerovice 131, CZ-54982 Vernerovice (Kralovehradecky)
t: 491 582 138   e: bert.mien@tiscali.cz
alanrogers.com/CZ4555   www.aktief.cz

Accommodation: ☑ Pitch   ☑ Mobile home/chalet   ○ Hotel/B&B   ☑ Apartment

Camping Aktief is a small, rural site on the outskirts of the village of Vernerovice. The site is located close to the Polish border, east of the Krkonose (Giant) Mountains. The spectacular rock formations of Adrspach and Teplice nad Metuji are close at hand. This is a small site with just 20 pitches (all with 6A electricity), located in a tranquil and protected area with many fruit trees. From the campsite there are fine views around the surrounding rolling meadows and hills. The friendly Dutch owners have developed Camping Aktief as an important hiking centre. Plenty of other activities are also organised here, and detailed walking and cycle routes are available (in Dutch). The owners, Bert and Mien van Kampen, are happy to share their knowledge of the local area, including a number of good restaurants. They also organise special tours, including visits to a local brewery and glassworks. Bikes, mountain bikes and fishing equipment are available for hire on site.

You might like to know

Eight-day hiking tour 'Pad door het Verloren Land' (Crossing the Lost Country) starting from the site, includes breakfast, luggage transports and overnight stays in the Czech Republic and Poland. The Adrspach-Teplice rock park holds mountain bike competitions.

- ☑ Walking notes or maps available
- ☑ Waymarked footpath – direct access from site
- ☑ Waymarked footpath within 1 km. of site
- ☑ Cycle trail – direct access from site
- ☑ Cycle trail access within 2 km. of site
- ☑ Mountain bike track within 2 km. of site
- ☑ Bicycle hire on site
- ☑ Accompanied hiking trips
- ○ Accompanied cycling trips
- ☑ Drying room for wet clothes/boots
- ○ Packed lunch service

Camping Frymburk

Frymburk 184, CZ-38279 Frymburk (Jihocesky)
t: 380 735 284 e: info@campingfrymburk.cz
alanrogers.com/CZ4720 www.campingfrymburk.cz

Accommodation: ☑ Pitch ☑ Mobile home/chalet ○ Hotel/B&B ○ Apartment

Facilities: Three immaculate toilet blocks with washbasins, preset showers (charged) and an en-suite bathroom with toilet, basin and shower. Facilities for disabled visitors. Launderette. Shop, restaurant and bar, takeaway (1/5-15/9). Motorcaravan services. Playground. Canoe, bicycle, pedalos, rowing boat and surfboard hire. Kidstown. Volleyball competitions. Rafting. Bus trips to Prague. Torches useful. Internet access and WiFi. Off site: Shops and restaurants in the village 900 m. from reception. Golf 7 km. Riding 15 km.

Open: 25 April - 21 September.

Directions: Take exit 114 at Passau in Germany (near Austrian border) towards Freyung in Czech Republic. Continue to Philipsreut, from there follow the no. 4 road towards Vimperk. Turn right a few kilometres after border towards Volary on no. 141 road. From Volary follow the no. 163 road to Horni Plana, Cerna and Frymburk. Site is on 163 road, right after village.

GPS: 48.655947, 14.170239

Charges guide

Per unit incl. 2 persons and electricity	CZK 460 - 810
extra person	CZK 80 - 130
child (2-11 yrs)	CZK 60 - 90
dog	CZK 50 - 60

No credit cards.
Less 20% 15/4-15/6 and 1/9-1/10.

Camping Frymburk is beautifully located on the Lipno lake in southern Bohemia and is an ideal site. From this site, activities could include walking, cycling, swimming, sailing, canoeing or rowing, and afterwards you could relax in the small, cosy bar/restaurant. You could enjoy a real Czech meal in one of the restaurants in Frymburk or on site. The site has 170 level pitches on terraces (all with 6A electricity, some with hardstanding and four have private sanitary units) and from the lower terraces on the edge of the lake there are lovely views over the water to the woods on the opposite side. A ferry crosses the lake from Frymburk where one can walk or cycle in the woods. The Dutch owner, Mr Wilzing, will welcome the whole family, personally siting your caravan. Children will be entertained by 'Kidstown' and the site has a small beach.

You might like to know

The cycle track from Frymburk to Lipno runs next to the site. It offers wonderful views of the lake and Frymburk, as well as a number of picnic spots.

☑ Walking notes or maps available
○ Waymarked footpath – direct access from site
☑ Waymarked footpath within 1 km. of site
☑ Cycle trail – direct access from site
○ Cycle trail access within 2 km. of site
○ Mountain bike track within 2 km. of site
☑ Bicycle hire on site
○ Accompanied hiking trips
○ Accompanied cycling trips
○ Drying room for wet clothes/boots
○ Packed lunch service

Facilities: Renovated toilet blocks with free hot showers. Washing and drying machine. Restaurant, takeaway and bar. Direct lake access with rowing boats and canoes. Heated indoor swimming pool with paddling pool (all season). Minigolf. Play area. Trampolines. Activity programme. Walking and cycling opportunities. WiFi throughout (free). Bicycle hire. Off site: Revnicov 2 km. with shops (including a supermarket), bars and restaurants. Fishing 3 km. Riding 4 km. Karlovy Vary 10 km. Prague 40 km. Koneprusy caves.

Open: 25 April - 15 September.

Directions: From the west, take no. 6/E48 express road towards Prague. Site is close to this road, 3 km. after the Revnicov exit and is clearly signed from this point. Coming from the east, ignore other camping signs and continue until Bucek is signed (to the north).

GPS: 50.1728, 13.8348

Charges guide

Per unit incl. 2 persons and electricity CZK 450 - 670

extra person CZK 75 - 100

child (under 12 yrs) CZK 50 - 75

dog CZK 50 - 60

Reductions in low season.
No credit cards.

Czech Republic – *Nové Straseci*

Camping Bucek

Trtice 170, CZ-27101 Nové Straseci (Stredocesky)
t: 313 564 212   e: info@campingbucek.cz
alanrogers.com/CZ4825   www.campingbucek.cz

Accommodation: ☑ Pitch   ☑ Mobile home/chalet   ○ Hotel/B&B   ☑ Apartment

Camping Bucek is a pleasant, Dutch-owned site 30 km. west of Prague. Its proprietors also own Camping Frymburk (CZ4720). Bucek is located on the edge of woodland and has direct access to a small lake with a private beach. Here you can enjoy canoes and rowing boats which are available to guests free of charge. There are 100 pitches here, many with pleasant views over the lake, and all with electrical connections (6A). Four pitches have their own private sanitary facilities. Shade is quite limited. On-site amenities include an indoor swimming pool, play equipment, trampolines and there is also an animation programme. A short distance from the site is a railway station from which you can catch a fast train into the centre of Prague. The castles of Karlstejn and Krivoklát are also within easy reach, along with Karlovy Vary.

You might like to know

The site is 5 km. from the small town of Nové Strašecí, with all services available there.

☑ Walking notes or maps available
○ Waymarked footpath – direct access from site
☑ Waymarked footpath within 1 km. of site
○ Cycle trail – direct access from site
☑ Cycle trail access within 2 km. of site
○ Mountain bike track within 2 km. of site
○ Bicycle hire on site
○ Accompanied hiking trips
○ Accompanied cycling trips
○ Drying room for wet clothes/boots
○ Packed lunch service

– Namestovo

Autocamping Stara Hora

Oravska Priehrada, SK-02901 Namestovo (Zilina)
t: 043 552 2223   e: camp.s.hora@stonline.sk
alanrogers.com/SK4905   www.oravskapriehrada.sk

Accommodation: ☑ Pitch ☑ Mobile home/chalet ○ Hotel/B&B ○ Apartment

Stara Hora has a beautiful location on the Orava artificial lake. It is in the northeast of Slovakia in the Tatra Mountains and attracts visitors from all over Europe which creates a happy and sometimes noisy atmosphere. The site has its own pebble beach with a large grass area behind it for sunbathing. Autocamping Stara Hora is on steeply sloping ground with 160 grassy pitches, all for touring units and with 10A electricity. The lower pitches are level and have good views over the lake, pitches at the top are mainly used by tents. The lake provides opportunities for fishing, boating and sailing and the area is good for hiking and cycling and in winter, it is a popular skiing area.

You might like to know

There are some wonderful walks around the lake – the site managers will be pleased to recommend popular routes.

- ☑ Walking notes or maps available
- ○ Waymarked footpath – direct access from site
- ☑ Waymarked footpath within 1 km. of site
- ○ Cycle trail – direct access from site
- ☑ Cycle trail access within 2 km. of site
- ○ Mountain bike track within 2 km. of site
- ○ Bicycle hire on site
- ○ Accompanied hiking trips
- ○ Accompanied cycling trips
- ○ Drying room for wet clothes/boots
- ○ Packed lunch service

Facilities: The modern toilet block has British style toilets, open washbasins and controllable hot showers (free). It could be pressed in high season and hot water to the showers is only available from 07.00-10.00 and from 19.00-22.00. Shop for basics. Bar and lakeside bar. Small restaurant. Basic playground (new playground planned). Pedalo, canoe and rowing boat hire. Water skiing. Fishing (with permit). Torch useful. Off site: Slanica Island.

Open: May - September.

Directions: From Ruzomberok take E77 road north towards Trstena. Turn left in Tvrdosin on the 520 road towards Námestovo. Site is on the right.

GPS: 49.359333, 19.555

Charges guide

Per person € 2,42	
child € 1,21	
pitch incl. car € 3,04	
electricity € 2,73	

Facilities:
One acceptable sanitary block to the side of the camping area, but in winter the facilities in the bungalow at the entrance are used. Cooking facilities. Badminton. Rest room with TV. Small games room. Covered barbecue. WiFi. Off site: Shop outside entrance. Swimming pool 1.5 km.

Open: All year.

Directions: Site is signed from E18 road (Zilina-Martin) in the village of Vrutky, 3 km. northwest of Martin. Turn south on the bend and follow signs to Martinské Hole.

GPS: 49.108492, 18.899467

Charges guide

Per unit incl. 2 persons
and electricity € 15,20 - € 17,60

extra person € 4,30	
child (6-10 yrs) € 2,60	
dog € 0,70 - € 1,30	

Autocamping Turiec

Kolonia hviezda 92, SK-03608 Martin (Zilina)
t: 043 428 4215   e: recepcia@autocampingturiec.sk
alanrogers.com/SK4910   www.autocampingturiec.sk

Accommodation: ⊘ Pitch ⊘ Mobile home/chalet ○ Hotel/B&B ○ Apartment

Turiec is situated in northeast Slovakia, 1.5 kilometres from the small village of Vrutky, four kilometres north of Martin, at the foot of the Lucanska Mala Fatra mountains and with castles nearby. This good site has views towards the mountains and is quiet and well maintained. Holiday activities include hiking in summer, skiing in winter, both downhill and cross-country. There is room for about 30 units on slightly sloping grass inside a circular tarmac road with some shade from tall trees. Electrical connections (6A) are available for all places. You will receive a friendly welcome from Viktor Matovcik and his wife Lydia. A wooden chalet by the side of the camping area has a TV rest room and a small games room. Down the hill is a splendid restaurant serving excellent food. English is spoken.

You might like to know

Turiec is located in a heavily wooded area at the foothills of the Martinské mountains, with miles of excellent walks close at hand.

- ⊘ Walking notes or maps available
- ○ Waymarked footpath – direct access from site
- ⊘ Waymarked footpath within 1 km. of site
- ○ Cycle trail – direct access from site
- ⊘ Cycle trail access within 2 km. of site
- ○ Mountain bike track within 2 km. of site
- ○ Bicycle hire on site
- ○ Accompanied hiking trips
- ○ Accompanied cycling trips
- ○ Drying room for wet clothes/boots
- ○ Packed lunch service

Been to any good campsites lately?
We have

You'll find them here...

The UK's market leading independent guides to the best campsites

... also here...

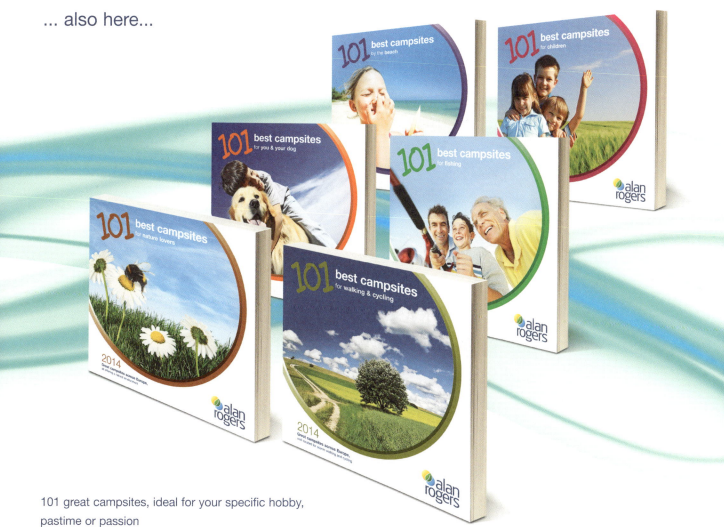

101 great campsites, ideal for your specific hobby, pastime or passion

Want independent campsite reviews at your fingertips?

You'll find them here...

Over 3,000 in-depth campsite reviews at **www.alanrogers.com**

...and even here...

FREE Alan Rogers bookstore app
- digital editions of all 2014 guides
alanrogers.com/digital

An exciting free app from iTunes
the Apple app store

Want to book your holiday on one of Europe's top campsites?

We can do it for you. No problem.

The best campsites in the most popular regions - we'll take care of everything

alan rogers travel

alan rogers

Discover the best campsites in Europe
with Alan Rogers

alanrogers.com
01580 214000

Index

Index

Index